ATHLETIC SCHOLARSHIP
24-MONTH
RECRUITING
PLANNER
AND JOURNAL

DELUXE EDITION

For High School Athletes and Parents

Your Personal All-In-One Resource for a
Successful Recruiting Experience

ATHLETIC SCHOLARSHIP SYSTEM

© 2020 Jon Fugler and Recruit-Me

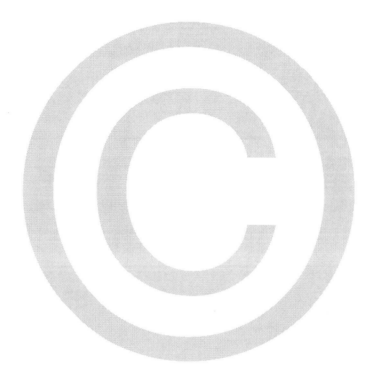

HOW TO USE THIS PLANNER AND JOURNAL

Welcome to The Recruit-Me Athletic Scholarship Planner and Journal. This is your all-in-one spot for your recruiting campaign.

You'll set your goals, calendar your strategy, plan your steps, document your efforts, and measure your results. This Journal and Planner is designed to help you make continual progress towards your goal of an athletic scholarship.

SECTION 1: Your real-time PLANNER AND JOURNAL PAGES are here. Set goals, fill in your calendar, then log your weekly progress. Ideally, you'll complete your written plan each week, but don't be alarmed if you skip a week here and there. This Planner is your friend, not a burdensome dictator.

SECTION 2: Your RECORD-KEEPING TOOLS are here. You'll want to refer to these pages throughout your recruiting experience.

SECTION 1: PLANNER & JOURNAL PAGES

This section walks you step-by-step through the next 24 months. Just complete the pages in order as you go. It's that easy.

 Set your goals for the next 12 months. In other words, what things do you want to accomplish by this time next year? Goal-setting is critical to your success. Writing them down is even more important.

 Fill in the first 12 months of your 24-month Calendar. Write in the key activities, such as school visits, camps, producing your video or other things you'll find on the Recruiting Checklist in the beginning of the Planner. You should update your calendar throughout the year.

 Fill in your Monthly Goals for the first month. Set 2–3 goals for this month. Otherwise, you'll wander. You need goals that are measurable and specific. At the end of the month, write down the results.

 Then set your goals for the next month.

 Fill in your Calendar for the first month. Now that you've set your goals for the month, complete your detailed monthly calendar. Fill in as much detail as you know. You can add to this calendar as new things arise.

 Fill in your Weekly Planner. This is where you win. Before you start the week, faithfully complete the top section. List up to three actions you'll take this week to achieve your goals. It is in your Weekly Planner where you'll make progress.

 At the end of every week, record the results of your week as indicated on your Weekly Planner page. And, while it's fresh in your mind, write down the actions you need to include in next week's plan. This will keep your momentum going. Then move onto the next week.

 At the end of every month, you'll find the Goal-Setting Page to get you started for the next month, followed by your Monthly Calendar and Weekly Planner.

This is *your* journal. Use it that way to document your feelings, attitudes, thoughts and actions. Putting this on paper is critical to your success. Make it a habit or you'll drop out of the race.

(Continued)

SECTION 2: RECORD-KEEPING TOOLS

Record-keeping tools in this section will allow you to log your activities and relationships. While the Section 1 is a chronological, running journal, the second section is a parking place for your critical data and activities. These pages will become your reference guide as you communicate with coaches, attend camps, keep a complete school list, visit schools, evaluate programs, and make your final school choice. There's even a scouting report for every school you communicate with.

My biggest piece of advice: write it down. That's what this Planner is all about. Some of the most successful people in the world keep journals and planners like this. They know how important it is to physically write things down.

May you find the Athletic Scholarship Recruiting Planner and Journal a gold mine for your scholarship pursuit.

Jon Fugler, CEO
Recruit-Me

Creator
The Recruit-Me Athletic Scholarship Planner

jon@recruit-me.com

RECRUITING CHECKLIST

1. Select the Right Schools to Contact
- ❑ Parents' desires and preferences. What's important? Write it down.
- ❑ Student-athlete's desires and preferences. What's important? Write it down.
- ❑ Parents' school list
- ❑ Student-Athlete's school list
- ❑ Discuss your lists or work together on one list
- ❑ Finalize list of 40–50 schools or more to contact
- ❑ Build chart with contact information

2. Build Your Introductory Packet & Questionnaire
- ❑ Cover letter
- ❑ Player Profile or Resume
- ❑ Questionnaire

3. Produce Your Video
- ❑ Personal introduction
- ❑ Highlights
- ❑ Continuous footage
- ❑ Edit and produce
- ❑ Post online
- ❑ Respond to coaches' requests

4. Track Your Communications
- ❑ Build a contact chart
- ❑ Columns for school, coach, phone, email, items you sent, video link sent, contact dates, and notes
- ❑ Journal your interactions with and communications to coaches in the contact dates and notes column
- ❑ Prepare questions to ask coaches
  - ❑ Athletic
  - ❑ Academic
  - ❑ College life
  - ❑ Financial

5. Build Your Updates
- ❑ One page with short, bulleted information
- ❑ When to send:
  - ❑ After every season
  - ❑ After every semester with updated grade info
  - ❑ After every SAT and ACT test
  - ❑ Send your schedule before any season

6. Choose the Right Camps, Showcases, & Tournaments
- ❑ Set your budget first
- ❑ Be selective and strategic for cost savings
- ❑ Identify recruiting camps vs. instructional
- ❑ Identify camps at schools where you have an interest
- ❑ Identify camps where multiple coaches will be in attendance, if possible
- ❑ Identify camps where coaches from your listed schools will be in attendance
- ❑ Attend showcases that will give you exposure to a large number of coaches

7. Register with the NCAA & NAIA Eligibility Centers
- ❑ Register at the beginning of your Junior year
- ❑ Set up an account
- ❑ Update "My Sports" section regularly
- ❑ Guidance counselor must send transcript after you have completed at least 6 semesters of high school

8. Academic Performance
- ❑ Read and understand the NCAA academic requirements
- ❑ Read and understand the academic requirements at the top schools on your list
- ❑ Raise your GPA
  - ❑ Study habits
  - ❑ Class attendance
  - ❑ Tutors
- ❑ Improve your SAT and ACT test scores
  - ❑ Get coaching
- ❑ Commit to excellence

9. Know the Recruiting Rules
- ❑ Recruiting calendar
- ❑ Read and be familiar with the NCAA Guide
- ❑ Read and be familiar with the NAIA Guide

To download this checklist, visit Recruit-Me.com/checklist

SCHOOL PROSPECT LIST

Create a healthy list of schools and take the initiative to contact them. Don't wait for coaches to come to you. You need to be proactive. That's the secret to getting on a coach's radar. Start with a list of 40–50 schools and update the list throughout the recruiting process.

1. ....
2. ....
3. ....
4. ....
5. ....
6. ....
7. ....
8. ....
9. ....
10. ....
11. ....
12. ....
13. ....
14. ....
15. ....
16. ....
17. ....
18. ....
19. ....
20. ....
21. ....
22. ....
23. ....
24. ....

25. ....
26. ....
27. ....
28. ....
29. ....
30. ....
31. ....
32. ....
33. ....
34. ....
35. ....
36. ....
37. ....
38. ....
39. ....
40. ....
41. ....
42. ....
43. ....
44. ....
45. ....
46. ....
47. ....
48. ....

49. _____
50. _____
51. _____
52. _____
53. _____
54. _____
55. _____
56. _____
57. _____
58. _____
59. _____
60. _____
61. _____
62. _____
63. _____
64. _____
65. _____
66. _____
67. _____
68. _____
69. _____
70. _____
71. _____
72. _____
73. _____
74. _____

75. _____
76. _____
77. _____
78. _____
79. _____
80. _____
81. _____
82. _____
83. _____
84. _____
85. _____
86. _____
87. _____
88. _____
89. _____
90. _____
91. _____
92. _____
93. _____
94. _____
95. _____
96. _____
97. _____
98. _____
99. _____
100. _____

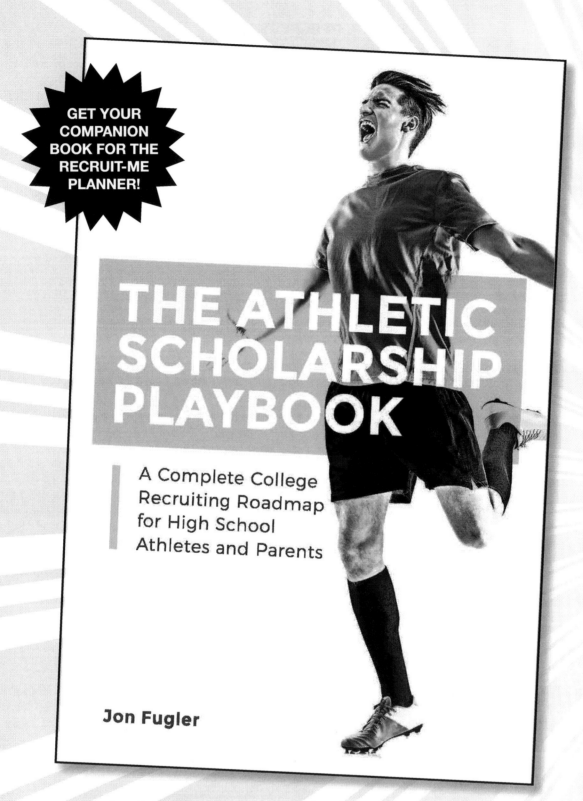

SECTION 1:
PLANNER AND
JOURNAL PAGES

"Action produces traction."

- JON FUGLER, ATHLETIC SCHOLARSHIP COACH

12-MONTH GOALS

What I will accomplish by this time next year

DATE: July 1, 20xx

GOALS:

Goals Met

1. Contact 70 schools by July 31 ☒
2. Achieve 3.2 GPA in First Semester ☐
3. Visit 8 schools by Sept. 30 ☒
4. Have 40 Phone conversations with Coaches ☐
5. 10 Coaches watch me compete ☐
6. Get invited to 2 Showcases ☐
7. Receive 5 offers by end of 12 months ☐

- Top Schools to Visit:

   - Stanford

   - New Mexico

   - UCLA   *Reminder to pursue them!*

   - UC Davis

- Research best camps for me

12-MONTH GOALS

What I will accomplish by this time next year

DATE: ⎯⎯⎯⎯⎯⎯⎯⎯⎯⎯

GOALS: **Goals Met**

1. ⎯⎯   ☐

2. ⎯⎯   ☐

3. ⎯⎯   ☐

4. ⎯⎯   ☐

5. ⎯⎯   ☐

6. ⎯⎯   ☐

7. ⎯⎯   ☐

APRIL	MAY	JUNE
15-Vist U of F	25-27 Soccer Tourney – Contact Coaches nearby	
JULY	**AUGUST**	**SEPTEMBER**
11-Visit USF 12 – Visit Sac State 18-19 Camp at U of Oregon	Send end-of-summer updates	
OCTOBER	**NOVEMBER**	**DECEMBER**
15 – DEADLINE! Application for Wash. St.	Take SATs	8 – Showcase in AZ
JANUARY	**FEBRUARY**	**MARCH**
10 – Send update to all Coaches 12 – Financial Aid Workshop		

12-MONTH CALENDAR

1-MONTH GOALS

GOALS	RESULTS
Contact 20 Schools	Achieved on 1/23!!
Update my Resume	(Have Dad proof it)
Register w/ Clearinghouses by 1/31	

NOTES:

# of Schools Contacted: ✗ ✗ ✗ 20 !

- Remember to update my website

1-MONTH GOALS

MO. _____

YR. _____

GOALS	RESULTS

NOTES:

1-MONTH CALENDAR

MO. May

YR. 20xx

SUN	MON	TUES	WED	THURS	FRI	SAT
		1	2 Call Coach Smith	3 7pm Update my Resume	4	5 8am SATs
6	7	8 Send 5 Intro Packets	9 7pm Coach Peters	10	11	12
13	14	15 Send 5 Intro Packets	16	17 7pm Call 3 Coaches	18 Tournament in Austin	19
20	21	22 Send 5 Intro Packets	23	24 Register w/ Eligibility Centers!!!	25	26 12pm Lunch w/ Mom and Dad – school list
27	28	29 Send 5 Intro Packets	30	31		

PLAN AHEAD! Update your calendar into the future.

MO. _____

YR. _____

1-MONTH CALENDAR

SUN	MON	TUES	WED	THURS	FRI	SAT

PLAN AHEAD! Update your calendar into the future.

WEEKLY PLANNER

Week Dates: May 5-11

My actions to take this week (in order of priority):

Action Taken

1. Finish my profile/resume ✗

2. Spend 30 minutes researching AUBURN ☐

3. ☐

A SUCCESS:	Had one of my best games of the year!
A SETBACK:	Creighton isn't interested
SOMETHING I LEARNED THIS WEEK:	I should have called Coach Green - DON'T WAIT to call coaches back!!!

Journal & Notes:

- I had a great practice Tuesday. It really helped me understand the new plays

- Don't forget to call coach at Alabama

- Check email daily

I need to include these actions in next week's plan:

1. Research these schools: Davidson, Cornell, Ohio State

2. Sign up for 2 camps

3. Ask Dad about my top choices - get his input!

WEEKLY PLANNER

Week Dates:

My actions to take this week (in order of priority):   **Action Taken**

1. ....   ☐

2. ....   ☐

3. ....   ☐

A SUCCESS:	
A SETBACK:	
SOMETHING I LEARNED THIS WEEK:	

Journal & Notes:

_____

_____

_____

_____

_____

_____

_____

_____

I need to include these actions in next week's plan:

1. ....

2. ....

3. ....

WEEKLY PLANNER

Week Dates: ....

My actions to take this week (in order of priority):

Action Taken

1. .... ☐

2. .... ☐

3. .... ☐

A SUCCESS:	
A SETBACK:	
SOMETHING I LEARNED THIS WEEK:	

Journal & Notes:

_____

_____

_____

_____

_____

_____

_____

_____

I need to include these actions in next week's plan:

1. ....

2. ....

3. ....

WEEKLY PLANNER

Week Dates:

My actions to take this week (in order of priority):

Action Taken

1. _____ ☐

2. _____ ☐

3. _____ ☐

A SUCCESS:	
A SETBACK:	
SOMETHING I LEARNED THIS WEEK:	

Journal & Notes:

_____

_____

_____

_____

_____

_____

_____

I need to include these actions in next week's plan:

1. _____

2. _____

3. _____

WEEKLY PLANNER

Week Dates:

My actions to take this week (in order of priority):

Action Taken

1. ☐

2. ☐

3. ☐

A SUCCESS:	
A SETBACK:	
SOMETHING I LEARNED THIS WEEK:	

Journal & Notes:

I need to include these actions in next week's plan:

1.

2.

3.

WEEKLY PLANNER

Week Dates: _____

My actions to take this week (in order of priority):   **Action Taken**

1. _____   ☐

2. _____   ☐

3. _____   ☐

A SUCCESS:	
A SETBACK:	
SOMETHING I LEARNED THIS WEEK:	

Journal & Notes:

_____

_____

_____

_____

_____

_____

_____

_____

I need to include these actions in next week's plan:

1. _____

2. _____

3. _____

1-MONTH GOALS

GOALS	RESULTS

NOTES:

MO. _____

YR. _____

1-MONTH CALENDAR

SUN	MON	TUES	WED	THURS	FRI	SAT

PLAN AHEAD! Update your calendar into the future.

WEEKLY PLANNER

Week Dates:

My actions to take this week (in order of priority):

Action Taken

1. ⬚

2. ⬚

3. ⬚

A SUCCESS:	
A SETBACK:	
SOMETHING I LEARNED THIS WEEK:	

Journal & Notes:

I need to include these actions in next week's plan:

1.

2.

3.

WEEKLY PLANNER

Week Dates:

My actions to take this week (in order of priority):   **Action Taken**

1. _____ ☐

2. _____ ☐

3. _____ ☐

A SUCCESS:	
A SETBACK:	
SOMETHING I LEARNED THIS WEEK:	

Journal & Notes:

_____

_____

_____

_____

_____

_____

_____

_____

I need to include these actions in next week's plan:

1. _____

2. _____

3. _____

WEEKLY PLANNER

Week Dates:

My actions to take this week (in order of priority):

Action Taken

1. ⬚

2. ⬚

3. ⬚

A SUCCESS:	
A SETBACK:	
SOMETHING I LEARNED THIS WEEK:	

Journal & Notes:

I need to include these actions in next week's plan:

1.

2.

3.

WEEKLY PLANNER

Week Dates:

My actions to take this week (in order of priority):   **Action Taken**

1. _____ ☐

2. _____ ☐

3. _____ ☐

A SUCCESS:	
A SETBACK:	
SOMETHING I LEARNED THIS WEEK:	

Journal & Notes:

_____

_____

_____

_____

_____

_____

_____

_____

I need to include these actions in next week's plan:

1. _____

2. _____

3. _____

WEEKLY PLANNER

Week Dates:

My actions to take this week (in order of priority):   **Action Taken**

1. ☐

2. ☐

3. ☐

A SUCCESS:	
A SETBACK:	
SOMETHING I LEARNED THIS WEEK:	

Journal & Notes:

I need to include these actions in next week's plan:

1.

2.

3.

1-MONTH GOALS

MO. _____

YR. _____

GOALS	RESULTS

NOTES:

_____

_____

_____

_____

_____

_____

_____

1-MONTH CALENDAR

MO. _____

YR. _____

SUN	MON	TUES	WED	THURS	FRI	SAT

PLAN AHEAD! Update your calendar into the future.

WEEKLY PLANNER

Week Dates:

My actions to take this week (in order of priority):   Action Taken

1. ☐

2. ☐

3. ☐

A SUCCESS:	
A SETBACK:	
SOMETHING I LEARNED THIS WEEK:	

Journal & Notes:

I need to include these actions in next week's plan:

1.

2.

3.

WEEKLY PLANNER

Week Dates: ....

My actions to take this week (in order of priority):   **Action Taken**

1. ....   ☐

2. ....   ☐

3. ....   ☐

A SUCCESS:	
A SETBACK:	
SOMETHING I LEARNED THIS WEEK:	

Journal & Notes:

....

....

....

....

....

....

....

....

I need to include these actions in next week's plan:

1. ....

2. ....

3. ....

WEEKLY PLANNER

Week Dates: _____

My actions to take this week (in order of priority):   **Action Taken**

1. _____   ☐

2. _____   ☐

3. _____   ☐

A SUCCESS:	
A SETBACK:	
SOMETHING I LEARNED THIS WEEK:	

Journal & Notes:

_____

_____

_____

_____

_____

_____

_____

I need to include these actions in next week's plan:

1. _____

2. _____

3. _____

WEEKLY PLANNER

Week Dates: ....

My actions to take this week (in order of priority):

Action Taken

1. .... ☐

2. .... ☐

3. .... ☐

A SUCCESS:	
A SETBACK:	
SOMETHING I LEARNED THIS WEEK:	

Journal & Notes:

....

....

....

....

....

....

....

I need to include these actions in next week's plan:

1. ....

2. ....

3. ....

WEEKLY PLANNER

Week Dates: _____

My actions to take this week (in order of priority):   **Action Taken**

1. _____   ☐

2. _____   ☐

3. _____   ☐

A SUCCESS:	
A SETBACK:	
SOMETHING I LEARNED THIS WEEK:	

Journal & Notes:

_____

_____

_____

_____

_____

_____

_____

_____

I need to include these actions in next week's plan:

1. _____

2. _____

3. _____

GOALS	RESULTS

NOTES:

_____

_____

_____

_____

_____

_____

_____

MO. _____

YR. _____

1-MONTH CALENDAR

SUN	MON	TUES	WED	THURS	FRI	SAT

PLAN AHEAD! Update your calendar into the future.

WEEKLY PLANNER

Week Dates:

My actions to take this week (in order of priority):　　　　　　　**Action Taken**

1. ....　☐

2. ....　☐

3. ....　☐

A SUCCESS:	
A SETBACK:	
SOMETHING I LEARNED THIS WEEK:	

Journal & Notes:

I need to include these actions in next week's plan:

1. ....

2. ....

3. ....

WEEKLY PLANNER

Week Dates: ....

My actions to take this week (in order of priority):   **Action Taken**

1. .... ☐

2. .... ☐

3. .... ☐

A SUCCESS:	
A SETBACK:	
SOMETHING I LEARNED THIS WEEK:	

Journal & Notes:

....

....

....

....

....

....

....

I need to include these actions in next week's plan:

1. ....

2. ....

3. ....

WEEKLY PLANNER

Week Dates:

My actions to take this week (in order of priority):
Action Taken

1. ☐

2. ☐

3. ☐

A SUCCESS:	
A SETBACK:	
SOMETHING I LEARNED THIS WEEK:	

Journal & Notes:

I need to include these actions in next week's plan:

1.

2.

3.

WEEKLY PLANNER

Week Dates:

My actions to take this week (in order of priority):   **Action Taken**

1. ☐

2. ☐

3. ☐

A SUCCESS:	
A SETBACK:	
SOMETHING I LEARNED THIS WEEK:	

Journal & Notes:

I need to include these actions in next week's plan:

1.

2.

3.

WEEKLY PLANNER

Week Dates:

My actions to take this week (in order of priority):   **Action Taken**

1.   ☐

2.   ☐

3.   ☐

A SUCCESS:	
A SETBACK:	
SOMETHING I LEARNED THIS WEEK:	

Journal & Notes:

I need to include these actions in next week's plan:

1.

2.

3.

1-MONTH GOALS

MO. _____

YR. _____

GOALS	RESULTS

NOTES:

_____

_____

_____

_____

_____

_____

_____

1-MONTH CALENDAR

MO. _____

YR. _____

SUN	MON	TUES	WED	THURS	FRI	SAT

PLAN AHEAD! Update your calendar into the future.

WEEKLY PLANNER

Week Dates:

My actions to take this week (in order of priority):   **Action Taken**

1. _____ ☐

2. _____ ☐

3. _____ ☐

A SUCCESS:	
A SETBACK:	
SOMETHING I LEARNED THIS WEEK:	

Journal & Notes:

_____

_____

_____

_____

_____

_____

_____

_____

I need to include these actions in next week's plan:

1. _____

2. _____

3. _____

WEEKLY PLANNER

Week Dates:

My actions to take this week (in order of priority):   **Action Taken**

1. ⬚

2. ⬚

3. ⬚

A SUCCESS:	
A SETBACK:	
SOMETHING I LEARNED THIS WEEK:	

Journal & Notes:

I need to include these actions in next week's plan:

1.

2.

3.

WEEKLY PLANNER

Week Dates:

My actions to take this week (in order of priority):

Action Taken

1. _____ ☐

2. _____ ☐

3. _____ ☐

A SUCCESS:	
A SETBACK:	
SOMETHING I LEARNED THIS WEEK:	

Journal & Notes:

_____

_____

_____

_____

_____

_____

_____

I need to include these actions in next week's plan:

1. _____

2. _____

3. _____

WEEKLY PLANNER

Week Dates: ....

My actions to take this week (in order of priority):   **Action Taken**

1. .... ☐

2. .... ☐

3. .... ☐

A SUCCESS:	
A SETBACK:	
SOMETHING I LEARNED THIS WEEK:	

Journal & Notes:

....

....

....

....

....

....

....

I need to include these actions in next week's plan:

1. ....

2. ....

3. ....

WEEKLY PLANNER

Week Dates: ....

My actions to take this week (in order of priority):   **Action Taken**

1. .... ☐

2. .... ☐

3. .... ☐

A SUCCESS:	
A SETBACK:	
SOMETHING I LEARNED THIS WEEK:	

Journal & Notes:

_____

_____

_____

_____

_____

_____

_____

I need to include these actions in next week's plan:

1. ....

2. ....

3. ....

1-MONTH GOALS

GOALS	RESULTS

NOTES:

MO. _____

YR. _____

1-MONTH CALENDAR

SUN	MON	TUES	WED	THURS	FRI	SAT

PLAN AHEAD! Update your calendar into the future.

WEEKLY PLANNER

Week Dates: ....

My actions to take this week (in order of priority):   **Action Taken**

1. .... ☐

2. .... ☐

3. .... ☐

A SUCCESS:	
A SETBACK:	
SOMETHING I LEARNED THIS WEEK:	

Journal & Notes:

....

....

....

....

....

....

....

I need to include these actions in next week's plan:

1. ....

2. ....

3. ....

WEEKLY PLANNER

Week Dates:

My actions to take this week (in order of priority):   **Action Taken**

1. _____ ☐

2. _____ ☐

3. _____ ☐

A SUCCESS:	
A SETBACK:	
SOMETHING I LEARNED THIS WEEK:	

Journal & Notes:

_____

_____

_____

_____

_____

_____

_____

_____

I need to include these actions in next week's plan:

1. _____

2. _____

3. _____

WEEKLY PLANNER

Week Dates: ....

My actions to take this week (in order of priority):　　　　　　**Action Taken**

1. ....　☐

2. ....　☐

3. ....　☐

A SUCCESS:	
A SETBACK:	
SOMETHING I LEARNED THIS WEEK:	

Journal & Notes:

....

....

....

....

....

....

....

I need to include these actions in next week's plan:

1. ....

2. ....

3. ....

WEEKLY PLANNER

Week Dates:

My actions to take this week (in order of priority):   **Action Taken**

1. .... ☐

2. .... ☐

3. .... ☐

A SUCCESS:	
A SETBACK:	
SOMETHING I LEARNED THIS WEEK:	

Journal & Notes:

_____

_____

_____

_____

_____

_____

_____

I need to include these actions in next week's plan:

1. _____

2. _____

3. _____

WEEKLY PLANNER

Week Dates: ....

My actions to take this week (in order of priority):
Action Taken

1. .... ☐

2. .... ☐

3. .... ☐

A SUCCESS:	
A SETBACK:	
SOMETHING I LEARNED THIS WEEK:	

Journal & Notes:

....

....

....

....

....

....

....

I need to include these actions in next week's plan:

1. ....

2. ....

3. ....

1-MONTH GOALS

MO. ....

YR. ....

GOALS	RESULTS

NOTES:

1-MONTH CALENDAR

MO. _____

YR. _____

SUN	MON	TUES	WED	THURS	FRI	SAT

PLAN AHEAD! Update your calendar into the future.

WEEKLY PLANNER

Week Dates:

My actions to take this week (in order of priority):   **Action Taken**

1. _____ ☐

2. _____ ☐

3. _____ ☐

A SUCCESS:	
A SETBACK:	
SOMETHING I LEARNED THIS WEEK:	

Journal & Notes:

_____

_____

_____

_____

_____

_____

_____

I need to include these actions in next week's plan:

1. _____

2. _____

3. _____

WEEKLY PLANNER

Week Dates: ....

My actions to take this week (in order of priority):   **Action Taken**

1. .... ☐

2. .... ☐

3. .... ☐

A SUCCESS:	
A SETBACK:	
SOMETHING I LEARNED THIS WEEK:	

Journal & Notes:

....

....

....

....

....

....

....

....

I need to include these actions in next week's plan:

1. ....

2. ....

3. ....

WEEKLY PLANNER

Week Dates:

My actions to take this week (in order of priority):   **Action Taken**

1. _____   ☐

2. _____   ☐

3. _____   ☐

A SUCCESS:	
A SETBACK:	
SOMETHING I LEARNED THIS WEEK:	

Journal & Notes:

_____

_____

_____

_____

_____

_____

_____

I need to include these actions in next week's plan:

1. _____

2. _____

3. _____

WEEKLY PLANNER

Week Dates:

My actions to take this week (in order of priority):   **Action Taken**

1. ☐

2. ☐

3. ☐

A SUCCESS:	
A SETBACK:	
SOMETHING I LEARNED THIS WEEK:	

Journal & Notes:

I need to include these actions in next week's plan:

1.

2.

3.

WEEKLY PLANNER

Week Dates:

My actions to take this week (in order of priority):   **Action Taken**

1. .... ☐

2. .... ☐

3. .... ☐

A SUCCESS:	
A SETBACK:	
SOMETHING I LEARNED THIS WEEK:	

Journal & Notes:

....

....

....

....

....

....

I need to include these actions in next week's plan:

1. ....

2. ....

3. ....

1-MONTH GOALS

GOALS	RESULTS

NOTES:

_____

_____

_____

_____

_____

_____

_____

MO. _____

YR. _____

1-MONTH CALENDAR

SUN	MON	TUES	WED	THURS	FRI	SAT

PLAN AHEAD! Update your calendar into the future.

WEEKLY PLANNER

Week Dates: ....

My actions to take this week (in order of priority):   **Action Taken**

1. .... ☐

2. .... ☐

3. .... ☐

A SUCCESS:	
A SETBACK:	
SOMETHING I LEARNED THIS WEEK:	

Journal & Notes:

....

....

....

....

....

....

....

I need to include these actions in next week's plan:

1. ....

2. ....

3. ....

WEEKLY PLANNER

Week Dates: _____

My actions to take this week (in order of priority):   **Action Taken**

1. _____ ☐

2. _____ ☐

3. _____ ☐

A SUCCESS:	
A SETBACK:	
SOMETHING I LEARNED THIS WEEK:	

Journal & Notes:

_____

_____

_____

_____

_____

_____

_____

I need to include these actions in next week's plan:

1. _____

2. _____

3. _____

WEEKLY PLANNER

Week Dates:

My actions to take this week (in order of priority):   **Action Taken**

1. ☐

2. ☐

3. ☐

A SUCCESS:	
A SETBACK:	
SOMETHING I LEARNED THIS WEEK:	

Journal & Notes:

I need to include these actions in next week's plan:

1.

2.

3.

WEEKLY PLANNER

Week Dates:

My actions to take this week (in order of priority):

Action Taken

1. ☐

2. ☐

3. ☐

A SUCCESS:	
A SETBACK:	
SOMETHING I LEARNED THIS WEEK:	

Journal & Notes:

I need to include these actions in next week's plan:

1.

2.

3.

WEEKLY PLANNER

Week Dates:

My actions to take this week (in order of priority):   **Action Taken**

1. .... ☐

2. .... ☐

3. .... ☐

A SUCCESS:	
A SETBACK:	
SOMETHING I LEARNED THIS WEEK:	

Journal & Notes:

_____

_____

_____

_____

_____

_____

_____

I need to include these actions in next week's plan:

1. ....

2. ....

3. ....

1-MONTH GOALS

MO. _____

YR. _____

GOALS	RESULTS

NOTES:

_____

_____

_____

_____

_____

_____

_____

1-MONTH CALENDAR

MO. _____

YR. _____

SUN	MON	TUES	WED	THURS	FRI	SAT

PLAN AHEAD! Update your calendar into the future.

WEEKLY PLANNER

Week Dates:

My actions to take this week (in order of priority):   **Action Taken**

1. .... ☐

2. .... ☐

3. .... ☐

A SUCCESS:	
A SETBACK:	
SOMETHING I LEARNED THIS WEEK:	

Journal & Notes:

....

....

....

....

....

....

....

....

I need to include these actions in next week's plan:

1. ....

2. ....

3. ....

WEEKLY PLANNER

Week Dates:

My actions to take this week (in order of priority):   **Action Taken**

1. .... ☐

2. .... ☐

3. .... ☐

A SUCCESS:	
A SETBACK:	
SOMETHING I LEARNED THIS WEEK:	

Journal & Notes:

....

....

....

....

....

....

....

I need to include these actions in next week's plan:

1. ....

2. ....

3. ....

WEEKLY PLANNER

Week Dates:

My actions to take this week (in order of priority):   **Action Taken**

1. ☐

2. ☐

3. ☐

A SUCCESS:	
A SETBACK:	
SOMETHING I LEARNED THIS WEEK:	

Journal & Notes:

I need to include these actions in next week's plan:

1.

2.

3.

WEEKLY PLANNER

Week Dates: ....

My actions to take this week (in order of priority):

Action Taken

1. .... ☐

2. .... ☐

3. .... ☐

A SUCCESS:	
A SETBACK:	
SOMETHING I LEARNED THIS WEEK:	

Journal & Notes:

....

....

....

....

....

....

....

I need to include these actions in next week's plan:

1. ....

2. ....

3. ....

WEEKLY PLANNER

Week Dates:

My actions to take this week (in order of priority):   **Action Taken**

1. ⬚

2. ⬚

3. ⬚

A SUCCESS:	
A SETBACK:	
SOMETHING I LEARNED THIS WEEK:	

Journal & Notes:

I need to include these actions in next week's plan:

1.

2.

3.

1-MONTH GOALS

GOALS	RESULTS

NOTES:

MO. _____

YR. _____

1-MONTH CALENDAR

SUN	MON	TUES	WED	THURS	FRI	SAT

PLAN AHEAD! Update your calendar into the future.

WEEKLY PLANNER

Week Dates: _____

My actions to take this week (in order of priority):   **Action Taken**

1. .... ☐

2. .... ☐

3. .... ☐

A SUCCESS:	
A SETBACK:	
SOMETHING I LEARNED THIS WEEK:	

Journal & Notes:

_____

_____

_____

_____

_____

_____

_____

I need to include these actions in next week's plan:

1. ....

2. ....

3. ....

WEEKLY PLANNER

Week Dates:

My actions to take this week (in order of priority):　　　　　　　**Action Taken**

1. .... ☐

2. .... ☐

3. .... ☐

A SUCCESS:	
A SETBACK:	
SOMETHING I LEARNED THIS WEEK:	

Journal & Notes:

....

....

....

....

....

....

I need to include these actions in next week's plan:

1. ....

2. ....

3. ....

WEEKLY PLANNER

Week Dates: ....

My actions to take this week (in order of priority):   **Action Taken**

1. .... ☐

2. .... ☐

3. .... ☐

A SUCCESS:	
A SETBACK:	
SOMETHING I LEARNED THIS WEEK:	

Journal & Notes:

....

....

....

....

....

....

....

I need to include these actions in next week's plan:

1. ....

2. ....

3. ....

WEEKLY PLANNER

Week Dates:

My actions to take this week (in order of priority):   **Action Taken**

1. _____   ☐

2. _____   ☐

3. _____   ☐

A SUCCESS:	
A SETBACK:	
SOMETHING I LEARNED THIS WEEK:	

Journal & Notes:

_____

_____

_____

_____

_____

_____

_____

_____

I need to include these actions in next week's plan:

1. _____

2. _____

3. _____

WEEKLY PLANNER

Week Dates: ....

My actions to take this week (in order of priority):   **Action Taken**

1. .... ☐

2. .... ☐

3. .... ☐

A SUCCESS:	
A SETBACK:	
SOMETHING I LEARNED THIS WEEK:	

Journal & Notes:

....

....

....

....

....

....

....

I need to include these actions in next week's plan:

1. ....

2. ....

3. ....

1-MONTH GOALS

MO. _____

YR. _____

GOALS	RESULTS

NOTES:

1-MONTH CALENDAR

MO. _____

YR. _____

SUN	MON	TUES	WED	THURS	FRI	SAT

PLAN AHEAD! Update your calendar into the future.

WEEKLY PLANNER

Week Dates:

My actions to take this week (in order of priority):   **Action Taken**

1. .... ☐

2. .... ☐

3. .... ☐

A SUCCESS:	
A SETBACK:	
SOMETHING I LEARNED THIS WEEK:	

Journal & Notes:

_____

_____

_____

_____

_____

_____

_____

I need to include these actions in next week's plan:

1. ....

2. ....

3. ....

WEEKLY PLANNER

Week Dates: ....

My actions to take this week (in order of priority):

Action Taken

1. .... ☐

2. .... ☐

3. .... ☐

A SUCCESS:	
A SETBACK:	
SOMETHING I LEARNED THIS WEEK:	

Journal & Notes:

....

....

....

....

....

....

....

....

I need to include these actions in next week's plan:

1. ....

2. ....

3. ....

WEEKLY PLANNER

Week Dates: ....

My actions to take this week (in order of priority):   **Action Taken**

1. .... ☐

2. .... ☐

3. .... ☐

A SUCCESS:	
A SETBACK:	
SOMETHING I LEARNED THIS WEEK:	

Journal & Notes:

....

....

....

....

....

....

....

I need to include these actions in next week's plan:

1. ....

2. ....

3. ....

WEEKLY PLANNER

Week Dates: ....

My actions to take this week (in order of priority):   **Action Taken**

1. .... ☐

2. .... ☐

3. .... ☐

A SUCCESS:	
A SETBACK:	
SOMETHING I LEARNED THIS WEEK:	

Journal & Notes:

....

....

....

....

....

....

....

I need to include these actions in next week's plan:

1. ....

2. ....

3. ....

WEEKLY PLANNER

Week Dates: ....

My actions to take this week (in order of priority):　　　　　　　　　**Action Taken**

1. .... ☐

2. .... ☐

3. .... ☐

A SUCCESS:	
A SETBACK:	
SOMETHING I LEARNED THIS WEEK:	

Journal & Notes:

....

....

....

....

....

....

....

I need to include these actions in next week's plan:

1. ....

2. ....

3. ....

1-MONTH GOALS

GOALS	RESULTS

NOTES:

MO. _____

YR. _____

1-MONTH CALENDAR

SUN	MON	TUES	WED	THURS	FRI	SAT

PLAN AHEAD! Update your calendar into the future.

WEEKLY PLANNER

Week Dates: ....

My actions to take this week (in order of priority):　　　　　　　**Action Taken**

1. ....　☐

2. ....　☐

3. ....　☐

A SUCCESS:	
A SETBACK:	
SOMETHING I LEARNED THIS WEEK:	

Journal & Notes:

....

....

....

....

....

....

....

I need to include these actions in next week's plan:

1. ....

2. ....

3. ....

WEEKLY PLANNER

Week Dates:

My actions to take this week (in order of priority):   **Action Taken**

1. _____   ☐

2. _____   ☐

3. _____   ☐

A SUCCESS:	
A SETBACK:	
SOMETHING I LEARNED THIS WEEK:	

Journal & Notes:

_____

_____

_____

_____

_____

_____

_____

I need to include these actions in next week's plan:

1. _____

2. _____

3. _____

WEEKLY PLANNER

Week Dates: ....

My actions to take this week (in order of priority):   **Action Taken**

1. .... ☐

2. .... ☐

3. .... ☐

A SUCCESS:	
A SETBACK:	
SOMETHING I LEARNED THIS WEEK:	

Journal & Notes:

....

....

....

....

....

....

....

....

I need to include these actions in next week's plan:

1. ....

2. ....

3. ....

WEEKLY PLANNER

Week Dates:

My actions to take this week (in order of priority):

Action Taken

1. ⬜

2. ⬜

3. ⬜

A SUCCESS:	
A SETBACK:	
SOMETHING I LEARNED THIS WEEK:	

Journal & Notes:

I need to include these actions in next week's plan:

1.

2.

3.

WEEKLY PLANNER

Week Dates:

My actions to take this week (in order of priority):   **Action Taken**

1. ☐

2. ☐

3. ☐

A SUCCESS:	
A SETBACK:	
SOMETHING I LEARNED THIS WEEK:	

Journal & Notes:

I need to include these actions in next week's plan:

1.

2.

3.

1-MONTH GOALS

MO. _____

YR. _____

GOALS	RESULTS

NOTES:

1-MONTH CALENDAR

MO. _____

YR. _____

SUN	MON	TUES	WED	THURS	FRI	SAT

PLAN AHEAD! Update your calendar into the future.

WEEKLY PLANNER

Week Dates:

My actions to take this week (in order of priority):

Action Taken

1. ⬚

2. ⬚

3. ⬚

A SUCCESS:	
A SETBACK:	
SOMETHING I LEARNED THIS WEEK:	

Journal & Notes:

I need to include these actions in next week's plan:

1.

2.

3.

WEEKLY PLANNER

Week Dates:

My actions to take this week (in order of priority):

Action Taken

1. ☐

2. ☐

3. ☐

A SUCCESS:	
A SETBACK:	
SOMETHING I LEARNED THIS WEEK:	

Journal & Notes:

I need to include these actions in next week's plan:

1.

2.

3.

WEEKLY PLANNER

Week Dates:

My actions to take this week (in order of priority):

Action Taken

1. ☐

2. ☐

3. ☐

A SUCCESS:	
A SETBACK:	
SOMETHING I LEARNED THIS WEEK:	

Journal & Notes:

I need to include these actions in next week's plan:

1.

2.

3.

WEEKLY PLANNER

Week Dates:

My actions to take this week (in order of priority):   **Action Taken**

1.   ☐

2.   ☐

3.   ☐

A SUCCESS:	
A SETBACK:	
SOMETHING I LEARNED THIS WEEK:	

Journal & Notes:

I need to include these actions in next week's plan:

1.

2.

3.

WEEKLY PLANNER

Week Dates: _____

My actions to take this week (in order of priority):   **Action Taken**

1. _____ ☐

2. _____ ☐

3. _____ ☐

A SUCCESS:	
A SETBACK:	
SOMETHING I LEARNED THIS WEEK:	

Journal & Notes:

_____

_____

_____

_____

_____

_____

_____

_____

I need to include these actions in next week's plan:

1. _____

2. _____

3. _____

1-MONTH GOALS

GOALS	RESULTS

NOTES:

1-MONTH CALENDAR

SUN	MON	TUES	WED	THURS	FRI	SAT

PLAN AHEAD! Update your calendar into the future.

WEEKLY PLANNER

Week Dates:

My actions to take this week (in order of priority):   **Action Taken**

1. .... ☐

2. .... ☐

3. .... ☐

A SUCCESS:	
A SETBACK:	
SOMETHING I LEARNED THIS WEEK:	

Journal & Notes:

_____

_____

_____

_____

_____

_____

_____

I need to include these actions in next week's plan:

1. _____

2. _____

3. _____

WEEKLY PLANNER

Week Dates: ....

My actions to take this week (in order of priority):

Action Taken

1. .... ☐

2. .... ☐

3. .... ☐

A SUCCESS:	
A SETBACK:	
SOMETHING I LEARNED THIS WEEK:	

Journal & Notes:

....

....

....

....

....

....

....

....

I need to include these actions in next week's plan:

1. ....

2. ....

3. ....

WEEKLY PLANNER

Week Dates:

My actions to take this week (in order of priority):

Action Taken

1. ⬜

2. ⬜

3. ⬜

A SUCCESS:	
A SETBACK:	
SOMETHING I LEARNED THIS WEEK:	

Journal & Notes:

I need to include these actions in next week's plan:

1.

2.

3.

WEEKLY PLANNER

Week Dates: ....

My actions to take this week (in order of priority):   **Action Taken**

1. .... ☐

2. .... ☐

3. .... ☐

A SUCCESS:	
A SETBACK:	
SOMETHING I LEARNED THIS WEEK:	

Journal & Notes:

....

....

....

....

....

....

....

....

I need to include these actions in next week's plan:

1. ....

2. ....

3. ....

PLANNER & JOURNAL SECOND 12 MONTHS

WEEKLY PLANNER

Week Dates: ....

My actions to take this week (in order of priority):   **Action Taken**

1. .... ☐

2. .... ☐

3. .... ☐

A SUCCESS:	
A SETBACK:	
SOMETHING I LEARNED THIS WEEK:	

Journal & Notes:

_____

_____

_____

_____

_____

_____

_____

I need to include these actions in next week's plan:

1. ....

2. ....

3. ....

1-MONTH GOALS

MO. _____

YR. _____

GOALS	RESULTS

NOTES:

1-MONTH CALENDAR

MO. _____

YR. _____

SUN	MON	TUES	WED	THURS	FRI	SAT

PLAN AHEAD! Update your calendar into the future.

WEEKLY PLANNER

Week Dates: ....

My actions to take this week (in order of priority):   **Action Taken**

1. .... ☐

2. .... ☐

3. .... ☐

A SUCCESS:	
A SETBACK:	
SOMETHING I LEARNED THIS WEEK:	

Journal & Notes:

....

....

....

....

....

....

....

....

I need to include these actions in next week's plan:

1. ....

2. ....

3. ....

WEEKLY PLANNER

Week Dates: _____

My actions to take this week (in order of priority):   **Action Taken**

1. _____ ☐

2. _____ ☐

3. _____ ☐

A SUCCESS:	
A SETBACK:	
SOMETHING I LEARNED THIS WEEK:	

Journal & Notes:

_____

_____

_____

_____

_____

_____

_____

_____

I need to include these actions in next week's plan:

1. _____

2. _____

3. _____

WEEKLY PLANNER

Week Dates: ....

My actions to take this week (in order of priority):　　　　　　　　　**Action Taken**

1. ....　☐

2. ....　☐

3. ....　☐

A SUCCESS:	
A SETBACK:	
SOMETHING I LEARNED THIS WEEK:	

Journal & Notes:

....

....

....

....

....

....

....

I need to include these actions in next week's plan:

1. ....

2. ....

3. ....

WEEKLY PLANNER

Week Dates:

My actions to take this week (in order of priority):   **Action Taken**

1. .... ☐

2. .... ☐

3. .... ☐

A SUCCESS:	
A SETBACK:	
SOMETHING I LEARNED THIS WEEK:	

Journal & Notes:

_____

_____

_____

_____

_____

_____

_____

I need to include these actions in next week's plan:

1. ....

2. ....

3. ....

WEEKLY PLANNER

Week Dates: ....

My actions to take this week (in order of priority):

Action Taken

1. .... ☐

2. .... ☐

3. .... ☐

A SUCCESS:	
A SETBACK:	
SOMETHING I LEARNED THIS WEEK:	

Journal & Notes:

....

....

....

....

....

....

....

....

I need to include these actions in next week's plan:

1. ....

2. ....

3. ....

1-MONTH GOALS

GOALS	RESULTS

NOTES:

1-MONTH CALENDAR

SUN	MON	TUES	WED	THURS	FRI	SAT

PLAN AHEAD! Update your calendar into the future.

WEEKLY PLANNER

Week Dates: ....

My actions to take this week (in order of priority):   **Action Taken**

1. .... ☐

2. .... ☐

3. .... ☐

A SUCCESS:	
A SETBACK:	
SOMETHING I LEARNED THIS WEEK:	

Journal & Notes:

....

....

....

....

....

....

....

I need to include these actions in next week's plan:

1. ....

2. ....

3. ....

WEEKLY PLANNER

Week Dates: ....

My actions to take this week (in order of priority):　　　　　　　　**Action Taken**

1. ....　☐

2. ....　☐

3. ....　☐

A SUCCESS:	
A SETBACK:	
SOMETHING I LEARNED THIS WEEK:	

Journal & Notes:

....

....

....

....

....

....

....

I need to include these actions in next week's plan:

1. ....

2. ....

3. ....

WEEKLY PLANNER

Week Dates: _____

My actions to take this week (in order of priority):   **Action Taken**

1. _____ ☐

2. _____ ☐

3. _____ ☐

A SUCCESS:	
A SETBACK:	
SOMETHING I LEARNED THIS WEEK:	

Journal & Notes:

_____

_____

_____

_____

_____

_____

_____

_____

I need to include these actions in next week's plan:

1. _____

2. _____

3. _____

WEEKLY PLANNER

Week Dates:

My actions to take this week (in order of priority):   **Action Taken**

1. _____ ☐

2. _____ ☐

3. _____ ☐

A SUCCESS:	
A SETBACK:	
SOMETHING I LEARNED THIS WEEK:	

Journal & Notes:

_____

_____

_____

_____

_____

_____

_____

_____

I need to include these actions in next week's plan:

1. _____

2. _____

3. _____

WEEKLY PLANNER

Week Dates: ....

My actions to take this week (in order of priority): **Action Taken**

1. .... ☐

2. .... ☐

3. .... ☐

A SUCCESS:	
A SETBACK:	
SOMETHING I LEARNED THIS WEEK:	

Journal & Notes:

....

....

....

....

....

....

....

....

I need to include these actions in next week's plan:

1. ....

2. ....

3. ....

1-MONTH GOALS

MO. _____

YR. _____

GOALS	RESULTS

NOTES:

1-MONTH CALENDAR

MO. _____

YR. _____

SUN	MON	TUES	WED	THURS	FRI	SAT

PLAN AHEAD! Update your calendar into the future.

WEEKLY PLANNER

Week Dates: ....

My actions to take this week (in order of priority):

Action Taken

1. .... ☐

2. .... ☐

3. .... ☐

A SUCCESS:	
A SETBACK:	
SOMETHING I LEARNED THIS WEEK:	

Journal & Notes:

....

....

....

....

....

....

....

I need to include these actions in next week's plan:

1. ....

2. ....

3. ....

WEEKLY PLANNER

Week Dates:

My actions to take this week (in order of priority):　　　　　　**Action Taken**

1. _____ ☐

2. _____ ☐

3. _____ ☐

A SUCCESS:	
A SETBACK:	
SOMETHING I LEARNED THIS WEEK:	

Journal & Notes:

_____

_____

_____

_____

_____

_____

_____

I need to include these actions in next week's plan:

1. _____

2. _____

3. _____

WEEKLY PLANNER

Week Dates: ....

My actions to take this week (in order of priority):

Action Taken

1. .... ☐

2. .... ☐

3. .... ☐

A SUCCESS:	
A SETBACK:	
SOMETHING I LEARNED THIS WEEK:	

Journal & Notes:

....

....

....

....

....

....

....

I need to include these actions in next week's plan:

1. ....

2. ....

3. ....

WEEKLY PLANNER

Week Dates: ....

My actions to take this week (in order of priority):   **Action Taken**

1. .... ☐

2. .... ☐

3. .... ☐

A SUCCESS:	
A SETBACK:	
SOMETHING I LEARNED THIS WEEK:	

Journal & Notes:

....

....

....

....

....

....

....

I need to include these actions in next week's plan:

1. ....

2. ....

3. ....

WEEKLY PLANNER

Week Dates: ....

My actions to take this week (in order of priority):   **Action Taken**

1. ....   ☐

2. ....   ☐

3. ....   ☐

A SUCCESS:	
A SETBACK:	
SOMETHING I LEARNED THIS WEEK:	

Journal & Notes:

....

....

....

....

....

....

....

....

I need to include these actions in next week's plan:

1. ....

2. ....

3. ....

1-MONTH GOALS

GOALS	RESULTS

NOTES:

_____

_____

_____

_____

_____

_____

_____

1-MONTH CALENDAR

SUN	MON	TUES	WED	THURS	FRI	SAT

PLANNER & JOURNAL **SECOND** 12 MONTHS

PLAN AHEAD! Update your calendar into the future.

WEEKLY PLANNER

Week Dates:

My actions to take this week (in order of priority):   **Action Taken**

1. .... ☐

2. .... ☐

3. .... ☐

A SUCCESS:	
A SETBACK:	
SOMETHING I LEARNED THIS WEEK:	

Journal & Notes:

_____

_____

_____

_____

_____

_____

_____

I need to include these actions in next week's plan:

1. ....

2. ....

3. ....

WEEKLY PLANNER

Week Dates: ....

My actions to take this week (in order of priority):   **Action Taken**

1. .... ☐

2. .... ☐

3. .... ☐

A SUCCESS:	
A SETBACK:	
SOMETHING I LEARNED THIS WEEK:	

Journal & Notes:

....

....

....

....

....

....

....

....

I need to include these actions in next week's plan:

1. ....

2. ....

3. ....

WEEKLY PLANNER

Week Dates:

My actions to take this week (in order of priority):   **Action Taken**

1. ☐

2. ☐

3. ☐

A SUCCESS:	
A SETBACK:	
SOMETHING I LEARNED THIS WEEK:	

Journal & Notes:

I need to include these actions in next week's plan:

1.

2.

3.

WEEKLY PLANNER

Week Dates:

My actions to take this week (in order of priority):   **Action Taken**

1. ☐

2. ☐

3. ☐

A SUCCESS:	
A SETBACK:	
SOMETHING I LEARNED THIS WEEK:	

Journal & Notes:

I need to include these actions in next week's plan:

1.

2.

3.

WEEKLY PLANNER

Week Dates:

My actions to take this week (in order of priority):   **Action Taken**

1. ☐

2. ☐

3. ☐

A SUCCESS:	
A SETBACK:	
SOMETHING I LEARNED THIS WEEK:	

Journal & Notes:

I need to include these actions in next week's plan:

1.

2.

3.

1-MONTH GOALS

MO. _____

YR. _____

GOALS	RESULTS

NOTES:

_____

_____

_____

_____

_____

_____

_____

PLANNER & JOURNAL **SECOND** 12 MONTHS

1-MONTH CALENDAR

MO. _____

YR. _____

SUN	MON	TUES	WED	THURS	FRI	SAT

PLAN AHEAD! Update your calendar into the future.

WEEKLY PLANNER

Week Dates:

My actions to take this week (in order of priority):   **Action Taken**

1. _____ ☐

2. _____ ☐

3. _____ ☐

A SUCCESS:	
A SETBACK:	
SOMETHING I LEARNED THIS WEEK:	

Journal & Notes:

_____

_____

_____

_____

_____

_____

_____

_____

I need to include these actions in next week's plan:

1. _____

2. _____

3. _____

WEEKLY PLANNER

Week Dates: ....

My actions to take this week (in order of priority):   **Action Taken**

1. .... ☐

2. .... ☐

3. .... ☐

A SUCCESS:	
A SETBACK:	
SOMETHING I LEARNED THIS WEEK:	

Journal & Notes:

....

....

....

....

....

....

....

I need to include these actions in next week's plan:

1. ....

2. ....

3. ....

WEEKLY PLANNER

Week Dates:

My actions to take this week (in order of priority):   **Action Taken**

1. ☐

2. ☐

3. ☐

A SUCCESS:	
A SETBACK:	
SOMETHING I LEARNED THIS WEEK:	

Journal & Notes:

I need to include these actions in next week's plan:

1.

2.

3.

WEEKLY PLANNER

Week Dates: ....

My actions to take this week (in order of priority):   **Action Taken**

1. .... ☐

2. .... ☐

3. .... ☐

A SUCCESS:	
A SETBACK:	
SOMETHING I LEARNED THIS WEEK:	

Journal & Notes:

....

....

....

....

....

....

....

I need to include these actions in next week's plan:

1. ....

2. ....

3. ....

WEEKLY PLANNER

Week Dates: _____

My actions to take this week (in order of priority):   **Action Taken**

1. _____ ☐

2. _____ ☐

3. _____ ☐

A SUCCESS:	
A SETBACK:	
SOMETHING I LEARNED THIS WEEK:	

Journal & Notes:

_____

_____

_____

_____

_____

_____

_____

_____

I need to include these actions in next week's plan:

1. _____

2. _____

3. _____

1-MONTH GOALS

GOALS	RESULTS

NOTES:

1-MONTH CALENDAR

SUN	MON	TUES	WED	THURS	FRI	SAT

PLAN AHEAD! Update your calendar into the future.

WEEKLY PLANNER

Week Dates:

My actions to take this week (in order of priority):   **Action Taken**

1. ☐

2. ☐

3. ☐

A SUCCESS:	
A SETBACK:	
SOMETHING I LEARNED THIS WEEK:	

Journal & Notes:

I need to include these actions in next week's plan:

1.

2.

3.

WEEKLY PLANNER

Week Dates:

My actions to take this week (in order of priority):   **Action Taken**

1. _____ ☐

2. _____ ☐

3. _____ ☐

A SUCCESS:	
A SETBACK:	
SOMETHING I LEARNED THIS WEEK:	

Journal & Notes:

_____

_____

_____

_____

_____

_____

_____

_____

I need to include these actions in next week's plan:

1. _____

2. _____

3. _____

WEEKLY PLANNER

Week Dates:

My actions to take this week (in order of priority):   **Action Taken**

1. ☐

2. ☐

3. ☐

A SUCCESS:	
A SETBACK:	
SOMETHING I LEARNED THIS WEEK:	

Journal & Notes:

I need to include these actions in next week's plan:

1.

2.

3.

WEEKLY PLANNER

Week Dates: _____

My actions to take this week (in order of priority):   **Action Taken**

1. _____ ☐

2. _____ ☐

3. _____ ☐

A SUCCESS:	
A SETBACK:	
SOMETHING I LEARNED THIS WEEK:	

Journal & Notes:

_____

_____

_____

_____

_____

_____

_____

I need to include these actions in next week's plan:

1. _____

2. _____

3. _____

WEEKLY PLANNER

Week Dates: ....

My actions to take this week (in order of priority):　　　　　　**Action Taken**

1. .... ☐

2. .... ☐

3. .... ☐

A SUCCESS:	
A SETBACK:	
SOMETHING I LEARNED THIS WEEK:	

Journal & Notes:

_____

_____

_____

_____

_____

_____

_____

I need to include these actions in next week's plan:

1. _____

2. _____

3. _____

1-MONTH GOALS

MO. _____

YR. _____

GOALS	RESULTS

NOTES:

_____

_____

_____

_____

_____

_____

_____

1-MONTH CALENDAR

MO. _____

YR. _____

SUN	MON	TUES	WED	THURS	FRI	SAT

PLAN AHEAD! Update your calendar into the future.

WEEKLY PLANNER

Week Dates: ....

My actions to take this week (in order of priority): **Action Taken**

1. .... ☐

2. .... ☐

3. .... ☐

A SUCCESS:	
A SETBACK:	
SOMETHING I LEARNED THIS WEEK:	

Journal & Notes:

_____

_____

_____

_____

_____

_____

_____

I need to include these actions in next week's plan:

1. ....

2. ....

3. ....

WEEKLY PLANNER

Week Dates:

My actions to take this week (in order of priority):   **Action Taken**

1. ☐

2. ☐

3. ☐

A SUCCESS:	
A SETBACK:	
SOMETHING I LEARNED THIS WEEK:	

Journal & Notes:

I need to include these actions in next week's plan:

1.

2.

3.

WEEKLY PLANNER

Week Dates: ....

My actions to take this week (in order of priority):

Action Taken

1. .... ☐

2. .... ☐

3. .... ☐

A SUCCESS:	
A SETBACK:	
SOMETHING I LEARNED THIS WEEK:	

Journal & Notes:

....

....

....

....

....

....

....

....

I need to include these actions in next week's plan:

1. ....

2. ....

3. ....

WEEKLY PLANNER

Week Dates: ....

My actions to take this week (in order of priority):   **Action Taken**

1. .... ☐

2. .... ☐

3. .... ☐

A SUCCESS:	
A SETBACK:	
SOMETHING I LEARNED THIS WEEK:	

Journal & Notes:

....

....

....

....

....

....

....

....

I need to include these actions in next week's plan:

1. ....

2. ....

3. ....

WEEKLY PLANNER

Week Dates: ....

My actions to take this week (in order of priority):   **Action Taken**

1. .... □

2. .... □

3. .... □

A SUCCESS:	
A SETBACK:	
SOMETHING I LEARNED THIS WEEK:	

Journal & Notes:

....

....

....

....

....

....

....

....

I need to include these actions in next week's plan:

1. ....

2. ....

3. ....

1-MONTH GOALS

GOALS	RESULTS

NOTES:

_____

_____

_____

_____

_____

_____

_____

MO. _____

YR. _____

1-MONTH CALENDAR

SUN	MON	TUES	WED	THURS	FRI	SAT

PLAN AHEAD! Update your calendar into the future.

WEEKLY PLANNER

Week Dates: ....

My actions to take this week (in order of priority):　　　　　　　**Action Taken**

1. ....　☐

2. ....　☐

3. ....　☐

A SUCCESS:	
A SETBACK:	
SOMETHING I LEARNED THIS WEEK:	

Journal & Notes:

....

....

....

....

....

....

....

....

I need to include these actions in next week's plan:

1. ....

2. ....

3. ....

WEEKLY PLANNER

Week Dates:

My actions to take this week (in order of priority):   **Action Taken**

1. _____ ☐

2. _____ ☐

3. _____ ☐

A SUCCESS:	
A SETBACK:	
SOMETHING I LEARNED THIS WEEK:	

Journal & Notes:

_____

_____

_____

_____

_____

_____

_____

I need to include these actions in next week's plan:

1. _____

2. _____

3. _____

WEEKLY PLANNER

Week Dates: ....

My actions to take this week (in order of priority): **Action Taken**

1. .... ☐

2. .... ☐

3. .... ☐

A SUCCESS:	
A SETBACK:	
SOMETHING I LEARNED THIS WEEK:	

Journal & Notes:

....

....

....

....

....

....

....

I need to include these actions in next week's plan:

1. ....

2. ....

3. ....

WEEKLY PLANNER

Week Dates: ....

My actions to take this week (in order of priority):   **Action Taken**

1. .... ☐

2. .... ☐

3. .... ☐

A SUCCESS:	
A SETBACK:	
SOMETHING I LEARNED THIS WEEK:	

Journal & Notes:

....

....

....

....

....

....

....

I need to include these actions in next week's plan:

1. ....

2. ....

3. ....

WEEKLY PLANNER

Week Dates: ....

My actions to take this week (in order of priority):　　　　　　　　　　**Action Taken**

1. .... ☐

2. .... ☐

3. .... ☐

A SUCCESS:	
A SETBACK:	
SOMETHING I LEARNED THIS WEEK:	

Journal & Notes:

....

....

....

....

....

....

....

I need to include these actions in next week's plan:

1. ....

2. ....

3. ....

1-MONTH GOALS

MO. _____

YR. _____

GOALS	RESULTS

NOTES:

1-MONTH CALENDAR

MO. _____

YR. _____

SUN	MON	TUES	WED	THURS	FRI	SAT

PLAN AHEAD! Update your calendar into the future.

WEEKLY PLANNER

Week Dates:

My actions to take this week (in order of priority):   **Action Taken**

1. ☐

2. ☐

3. ☐

A SUCCESS:	
A SETBACK:	
SOMETHING I LEARNED THIS WEEK:	

Journal & Notes:

I need to include these actions in next week's plan:

1.

2.

3.

WEEKLY PLANNER

Week Dates:

My actions to take this week (in order of priority):　　　　　**Action Taken**

1. _____ ☐

2. _____ ☐

3. _____ ☐

A SUCCESS:	
A SETBACK:	
SOMETHING I LEARNED THIS WEEK:	

Journal & Notes:

_____

_____

_____

_____

_____

_____

_____

I need to include these actions in next week's plan:

1. _____

2. _____

3. _____

WEEKLY PLANNER

Week Dates:

My actions to take this week (in order of priority):

Action Taken

1. _____ ☐

2. _____ ☐

3. _____ ☐

A SUCCESS:	
A SETBACK:	
SOMETHING I LEARNED THIS WEEK:	

Journal & Notes:

_____

_____

_____

_____

_____

_____

_____

I need to include these actions in next week's plan:

1. _____

2. _____

3. _____

WEEKLY PLANNER

Week Dates: ....

My actions to take this week (in order of priority):   **Action Taken**

1. .... ☐

2. .... ☐

3. .... ☐

A SUCCESS:	
A SETBACK:	
SOMETHING I LEARNED THIS WEEK:	

Journal & Notes:

....

....

....

....

....

....

....

....

I need to include these actions in next week's plan:

1. ....

2. ....

3. ....

WEEKLY PLANNER

Week Dates: ....

My actions to take this week (in order of priority):   **Action Taken**

1. .... ☐

2. .... ☐

3. .... ☐

A SUCCESS:	
A SETBACK:	
SOMETHING I LEARNED THIS WEEK:	

Journal & Notes:

....

....

....

....

....

....

....

I need to include these actions in next week's plan:

1. ....

2. ....

3. ....

1-MONTH GOALS

GOALS	RESULTS

NOTES:

_____

_____

_____

_____

_____

_____

MO. _____

YR. _____

1-MONTH CALENDAR

SUN	MON	TUES	WED	THURS	FRI	SAT

PLAN AHEAD! Update your calendar into the future.

WEEKLY PLANNER

Week Dates: ....

My actions to take this week (in order of priority):

Action Taken

1. .... ☐

2. .... ☐

3. .... ☐

A SUCCESS:	
A SETBACK:	
SOMETHING I LEARNED THIS WEEK:	

Journal & Notes:

....

....

....

....

....

....

....

I need to include these actions in next week's plan:

1. ....

2. ....

3. ....

WEEKLY PLANNER

Week Dates: ....

My actions to take this week (in order of priority):   **Action Taken**

1. ....   ☐

2. ....   ☐

3. ....   ☐

A SUCCESS:	
A SETBACK:	
SOMETHING I LEARNED THIS WEEK:	

Journal & Notes:

....

....

....

....

....

....

....

I need to include these actions in next week's plan:

1. ....

2. ....

3. ....

WEEKLY PLANNER

Week Dates:

My actions to take this week (in order of priority):

Action Taken

1. ☐

2. ☐

3. ☐

A SUCCESS:	
A SETBACK:	
SOMETHING I LEARNED THIS WEEK:	

Journal & Notes:

I need to include these actions in next week's plan:

1.

2.

3.

WEEKLY PLANNER

Week Dates: ....

My actions to take this week (in order of priority):   **Action Taken**

1. ....   ☐

2. ....   ☐

3. ....   ☐

A SUCCESS:	
A SETBACK:	
SOMETHING I LEARNED THIS WEEK:	

Journal & Notes:

....

....

....

....

....

....

....

....

I need to include these actions in next week's plan:

1. ....

2. ....

3. ....

WEEKLY PLANNER

Week Dates: ....

My actions to take this week (in order of priority):   **Action Taken**

1. .... ☐

2. .... ☐

3. .... ☐

A SUCCESS:	
A SETBACK:	
SOMETHING I LEARNED THIS WEEK:	

Journal & Notes:

....

....

....

....

....

....

....

....

I need to include these actions in next week's plan:

1. ....

2. ....

3. ....

SECTION 2:
RECORD-KEEPING TOOLS

"Everyone *wants* to be the best,
but few are willing to put in the
work to *be* the best."

- ERIK JOHNSON, HIGH SCHOOL SUPER-COACH

QUESTIONS FOR COACHES

QUESTIONS	ANSWERS

QUESTIONS	ANSWERS

COACH QUESTIONS

QUESTIONS	ANSWERS

QUESTIONS	ANSWERS

QUESTIONS FOR COACHES

QUESTIONS	ANSWERS

QUESTIONS	ANSWERS

QUESTIONS	ANSWERS

QUESTIONS	ANSWERS

COACH QUESTIONS

QUESTIONS	ANSWERS

QUESTIONS	ANSWERS

COACH QUESTIONS

QUESTIONS	ANSWERS

QUESTIONS	ANSWERS

COACH QUESTIONS

QUESTIONS	ANSWERS

QUESTIONS	ANSWERS

COACH QUESTIONS

COACHES WE'VE ENGAGED WITH

Build your list as you go

1. _____
2. _____
3. _____
4. _____
5. _____
6. _____
7. _____
8. _____
9. _____
10. _____
11. _____
12. _____
13. _____
14. _____
15. _____
16. _____
17. _____
18. _____
19. _____
20. _____
21. _____
22. _____
23. _____
24. _____
25. _____

26. _____
27. _____
28. _____
29. _____
30. _____
31. _____
32. _____
33. _____
34. _____
35. _____
36. _____
37. _____
38. _____
39. _____
40. _____
41. _____
42. _____
43. _____
44. _____
45. _____
46. _____
47. _____
48. _____
49. _____
50. _____

51. _____
52. _____
53. _____
54. _____
55. _____
56. _____
57. _____
58. _____
59. _____
60. _____
61. _____
62. _____
63. _____
64. _____
65. _____
66. _____
67. _____
68. _____
69. _____
70. _____
71. _____
72. _____
73. _____
74. _____
75. _____

76. _____
77. _____
78. _____
79. _____
80. _____
81. _____
82. _____
83. _____
84. _____
85. _____
86. _____
87. _____
88. _____
89. _____
90. _____
91. _____
92. _____
93. _____
94. _____
95. _____
96. _____
97. _____
98. _____
99. _____
100. _____

COACH ENGAGEMENT

HELP YOURSELF TO AN
ATHLETIC SCHOLARSHIP

ATHLETIC SCHOLARSHIP SYSTEM

A PROVEN STEP-BY-STEP SOLUTION

"I recommend Recruit-Me to anyone who is seeking guidance on how to navigate the recruiting process."

- Ernie W., Parent from Georgia

GET INSTANT ACCESS AT:
www.recruit-me.com/system

COACH CONVERSATIONS & INTERACTIONS

Keep a log of every conversation and interaction. Transfer main points
to the Communication Record of that school.

DATE	COACH & SCHOOL	MAIN POINTS	NEXT STEP
5/11	Jerry Andrews U of Conn.	– Send Video Link – Come visit his campus	Finish my video
5/15	Bill Williams Fordham	He wanted to see if I am still interested	Send him an update
5/21	Dan White West VA	I asked about openings he is filling. He is interested.	Send resume again!
5/27	Aaron Stover Vermont	He called me!!! Seems interested	Call him next week to show interest
6/2	Amy Harrison Tennessee	Emailed me about camp	Write back with Qs about camp

COACH CONVERSATIONS & INTERACTIONS

Keep a log of every conversation and interaction. Transfer main points
to the Communication Record of that school.

DATE	COACH & SCHOOL	MAIN POINTS	NEXT STEP

COACH CONVERSATIONS & INTERACTIONS

Keep a log of every conversation and interaction. Transfer main points
to the Communication Record of that school.

DATE	COACH & SCHOOL	MAIN POINTS	NEXT STEP

COACH INTERACTIONS

COACH CONVERSATIONS & INTERACTIONS

Keep a log of every conversation and interaction. Transfer main points
to the Communication Record of that school.

DATE	COACH & SCHOOL	MAIN POINTS	NEXT STEP

COACH CONVERSATIONS & INTERACTIONS

Keep a log of every conversation and interaction. Transfer main points
to the Communication Record of that school.

DATE	COACH & SCHOOL	MAIN POINTS	NEXT STEP

COACH INTERACTIONS

COACH CONVERSATIONS & INTERACTIONS

Keep a log of every conversation and interaction. Transfer main points
to the Communication Record of that school.

DATE	COACH & SCHOOL	MAIN POINTS	NEXT STEP

COACH CONVERSATIONS & INTERACTIONS

Keep a log of every conversation and interaction. Transfer main points
to the Communication Record of that school.

DATE	COACH & SCHOOL	MAIN POINTS	NEXT STEP

COACH CONVERSATIONS & INTERACTIONS

Keep a log of every conversation and interaction. Transfer main points
to the Communication Record of that school.

DATE	COACH & SCHOOL	MAIN POINTS	NEXT STEP

COACH CONVERSATIONS & INTERACTIONS

Keep a log of every conversation and interaction. Transfer main points
to the Communication Record of that school.

DATE	COACH & SCHOOL	MAIN POINTS	NEXT STEP

COACH INTERACTIONS

COACH CONVERSATIONS & INTERACTIONS

Keep a log of every conversation and interaction. Transfer main points
to the Communication Record of that school.

DATE	COACH & SCHOOL	MAIN POINTS	NEXT STEP

COACH CONVERSATIONS & INTERACTIONS

Keep a log of every conversation and interaction. Transfer main points
to the Communication Record of that school.

DATE	COACH & SCHOOL	MAIN POINTS	NEXT STEP

COACH INTERACTIONS

COACH CONVERSATIONS & INTERACTIONS

Keep a log of every conversation and interaction. Transfer main points
to the Communication Record of that school.

DATE	COACH & SCHOOL	MAIN POINTS	NEXT STEP

COACH CONVERSATIONS & INTERACTIONS

Keep a log of every conversation and interaction. Transfer main points
to the Communication Record of that school.

DATE	COACH & SCHOOL	MAIN POINTS	NEXT STEP

COACH CONVERSATIONS & INTERACTIONS

Keep a log of every conversation and interaction. Transfer main points
to the Communication Record of that school.

DATE	COACH & SCHOOL	MAIN POINTS	NEXT STEP

COACH CONVERSATIONS & INTERACTIONS

Keep a log of every conversation and interaction. Transfer main points
to the Communication Record of that school.

DATE	COACH & SCHOOL	MAIN POINTS	NEXT STEP

COACH CONVERSATIONS & INTERACTIONS

Keep a log of every conversation and interaction. Transfer main points
to the Communication Record of that school.

DATE	COACH & SCHOOL	MAIN POINTS	NEXT STEP

COACH CONVERSATIONS & INTERACTIONS

Keep a log of every conversation and interaction. Transfer main points
to the Communication Record of that school.

DATE	COACH & SCHOOL	MAIN POINTS	NEXT STEP

COACH INTERACTIONS

COACH CONVERSATIONS & INTERACTIONS

Keep a log of every conversation and interaction. Transfer main points
to the Communication Record of that school.

DATE	COACH & SCHOOL	MAIN POINTS	NEXT STEP

COACH CONVERSATIONS & INTERACTIONS

Keep a log of every conversation and interaction. Transfer main points
to the Communication Record of that school.

DATE	COACH & SCHOOL	MAIN POINTS	NEXT STEP

COACH INTERACTIONS

COACH CONVERSATIONS & INTERACTIONS

Keep a log of every conversation and interaction. Transfer main points
to the Communication Record of that school.

DATE	COACH & SCHOOL	MAIN POINTS	NEXT STEP

COACH CONVERSATIONS & INTERACTIONS

Keep a log of every conversation and interaction. Transfer main points
to the Communication Record of that school.

DATE	COACH & SCHOOL	MAIN POINTS	NEXT STEP

COACH INTERACTIONS

COMMUNICATION RECORD

SCHOOL: University of Connecticut

COACH	CONTACT INFO	MY INTEREST LEVEL (1-5)
Jerry Andrews	815-433-7112 jandrews@uconn.edu @jerryandrewscoach	3

DATE SENT INTRO PKT.	DATE COMPLETED QUESTIONNAIRE	DATE SENT VIDEO LINK	DATES SENT UPDATES
7/11	7/20	8/5	

DATES	CONTACTS & NOTES
8/19	Met Asst. Coach on visit to campus
8/20	Spent time w/ Admissions
9/4	He asked me to fill out ONLINE form
10/7	Sent my latest SAT Scores
10/15	Invited me for official visit!

SCOUTING REPORT

Keep an ongoing scouting report on every school/program you are engaged with.
Consider: Athletics, Academics, Coaching Staff, Campus, Finances, and other priorities you have.

STRENGTHS:	WEAKNESSES:
Winning program	Expensive
Good Coaches	Facilities
Strong Biology Major/Department	Many Seniors graduating, may affect
Big Campus	overall talent
Close to Home	
They are pursuing me - Good recruiting program	

SCHOOL REPORT CARD

SCHOOL REPORT CARD	RATING
Net Cost After All Financial Aid	$12,000/yr.
Athletic Scholarship Offer	$18,000/yr. → (Not confirmed yet!)
Athletic Quality	B
Academic Match	A
Quality of Program	B+
Coaching Staff	A
Coach's Interest Level in Me	A
Potential for My Improvement	A
Potential to Start in 1-2 Years	A
Overall Impression	B+

COMMUNICATION RECORD

SCHOOL: ....

COACH	CONTACT INFO	MY INTEREST LEVEL (1-5)

DATE SENT INTRO PKT.	DATE COMPLETED QUESTIONNAIRE	DATE SENT VIDEO LINK	DATES SENT UPDATES

DATES	CONTACTS & NOTES

SCOUTING REPORT

Keep an ongoing scouting report on every school/program you are engaged with.
Consider: Athletics, Academics, Coaching Staff, Campus, Finances, and other priorities you have.

STRENGTHS:	WEAKNESSES:

SCHOOL REPORT CARD

SCHOOL REPORT CARD	RATING
Net Cost After All Financial Aid	
Athletic Scholarship Offer	
Athletic Quality	
Academic Match	
Quality of Program	
Coaching Staff	
Coach's Interest Level in Me	
Potential for My Improvement	
Potential to Start in 1-2 Years	
Overall Impression	

COMMUNICATION RECORD

SCHOOL:

COACH	CONTACT INFO	MY INTEREST LEVEL (1-5)

DATE SENT INTRO PKT.	DATE COMPLETED QUESTIONNAIRE	DATE SENT VIDEO LINK	DATES SENT UPDATES

DATES	CONTACTS & NOTES

SCOUTING REPORT

Keep an ongoing scouting report on every school/program you are engaged with.
Consider: Athletics, Academics, Coaching Staff, Campus, Finances, and other priorities you have.

STRENGTHS:	WEAKNESSES:

SCHOOL REPORT CARD

SCHOOL REPORT CARD	RATING
Net Cost After All Financial Aid	
Athletic Scholarship Offer	
Athletic Quality	
Academic Match	
Quality of Program	
Coaching Staff	
Coach's Interest Level in Me	
Potential for My Improvement	
Potential to Start in 1-2 Years	
Overall Impression	

COMMUNICATION RECORD

SCHOOL: ....

COACH	CONTACT INFO	MY INTEREST LEVEL (1-5)

DATE SENT INTRO PKT.	DATE COMPLETED QUESTIONNAIRE	DATE SENT VIDEO LINK	DATES SENT UPDATES

DATES	CONTACTS & NOTES

SCOUTING REPORT

Keep an ongoing scouting report on every school/program you are engaged with.
Consider: Athletics, Academics, Coaching Staff, Campus, Finances, and other priorities you have.

STRENGTHS:	WEAKNESSES:

SCHOOL REPORT CARD

SCHOOL REPORT CARD	RATING
Net Cost After All Financial Aid	
Athletic Scholarship Offer	
Athletic Quality	
Academic Match	
Quality of Program	
Coaching Staff	
Coach's Interest Level in Me	
Potential for My Improvement	
Potential to Start in 1-2 Years	
Overall Impression	

COMMUNICATION RECORD

SCHOOL: ....

COACH	CONTACT INFO	MY INTEREST LEVEL (1-5)

DATE SENT INTRO PKT.	DATE COMPLETED QUESTIONNAIRE	DATE SENT VIDEO LINK	DATES SENT UPDATES

DATES	CONTACTS & NOTES

SCOUTING REPORT

Keep an ongoing scouting report on every school/program you are engaged with.
Consider: Athletics, Academics, Coaching Staff, Campus, Finances, and other priorities you have.

STRENGTHS:	WEAKNESSES:

SCHOOL REPORT CARD

SCHOOL REPORT CARD	RATING
Net Cost After All Financial Aid	
Athletic Scholarship Offer	
Athletic Quality	
Academic Match	
Quality of Program	
Coaching Staff	
Coach's Interest Level in Me	
Potential for My Improvement	
Potential to Start in 1-2 Years	
Overall Impression	

COMMUNICATION RECORD

SCHOOL: ....

COACH	CONTACT INFO	MY INTEREST LEVEL (1-5)

DATE SENT INTRO PKT.	DATE COMPLETED QUESTIONNAIRE	DATE SENT VIDEO LINK	DATES SENT UPDATES

DATES	CONTACTS & NOTES

SCOUTING REPORT

Keep an ongoing scouting report on every school/program you are engaged with.
Consider: Athletics, Academics, Coaching Staff, Campus, Finances, and other priorities you have.

STRENGTHS:	WEAKNESSES:

SCHOOL REPORT CARD

SCHOOL REPORT CARD	RATING
Net Cost After All Financial Aid	
Athletic Scholarship Offer	
Athletic Quality	
Academic Match	
Quality of Program	
Coaching Staff	
Coach's Interest Level in Me	
Potential for My Improvement	
Potential to Start in 1-2 Years	
Overall Impression	

COMMUNICATION RECORD

SCHOOL:

COACH	CONTACT INFO	MY INTEREST LEVEL (1-5)

DATE SENT INTRO PKT.	DATE COMPLETED QUESTIONNAIRE	DATE SENT VIDEO LINK	DATES SENT UPDATES

DATES	CONTACTS & NOTES

SCOUTING REPORT

Keep an ongoing scouting report on every school/program you are engaged with.
Consider: Athletics, Academics, Coaching Staff, Campus, Finances, and other priorities you have.

STRENGTHS:	WEAKNESSES:

SCHOOL REPORT CARD

SCHOOL REPORT CARD	RATING
Net Cost After All Financial Aid	
Athletic Scholarship Offer	
Athletic Quality	
Academic Match	
Quality of Program	
Coaching Staff	
Coach's Interest Level in Me	
Potential for My Improvement	
Potential to Start in 1-2 Years	
Overall Impression	

COMMUNICATION RECORD

SCHOOL:

COACH	CONTACT INFO	MY INTEREST LEVEL (1-5)

DATE SENT INTRO PKT.	DATE COMPLETED QUESTIONNAIRE	DATE SENT VIDEO LINK	DATES SENT UPDATES

DATES	CONTACTS & NOTES

SCOUTING REPORT

Keep an ongoing scouting report on every school/program you are engaged with.
Consider: Athletics, Academics, Coaching Staff, Campus, Finances, and other priorities you have.

STRENGTHS:	WEAKNESSES:

SCHOOL REPORT CARD

SCHOOL REPORT CARD	RATING
Net Cost After All Financial Aid	
Athletic Scholarship Offer	
Athletic Quality	
Academic Match	
Quality of Program	
Coaching Staff	
Coach's Interest Level in Me	
Potential for My Improvement	
Potential to Start in 1-2 Years	
Overall Impression	

COMMUNICATION RECORD

SCHOOL:

COACH	CONTACT INFO	MY INTEREST LEVEL (1-5)

DATE SENT INTRO PKT.	DATE COMPLETED QUESTIONNAIRE	DATE SENT VIDEO LINK	DATES SENT UPDATES

DATES	CONTACTS & NOTES

SCOUTING REPORT

Keep an ongoing scouting report on every school/program you are engaged with.
Consider: Athletics, Academics, Coaching Staff, Campus, Finances, and other priorities you have.

STRENGTHS:	WEAKNESSES:

SCHOOL REPORT CARD

SCHOOL REPORT CARD	RATING
Net Cost After All Financial Aid	
Athletic Scholarship Offer	
Athletic Quality	
Academic Match	
Quality of Program	
Coaching Staff	
Coach's Interest Level in Me	
Potential for My Improvement	
Potential to Start in 1-2 Years	
Overall Impression	

COMMUNICATION RECORD

SCHOOL: _____

COACH	CONTACT INFO	MY INTEREST LEVEL (1-5)

DATE SENT INTRO PKT.	DATE COMPLETED QUESTIONNAIRE	DATE SENT VIDEO LINK	DATES SENT UPDATES

DATES	CONTACTS & NOTES

SCOUTING REPORT

Keep an ongoing scouting report on every school/program you are engaged with.
Consider: Athletics, Academics, Coaching Staff, Campus, Finances, and other priorities you have.

STRENGTHS:	WEAKNESSES:

SCHOOL REPORT CARD

SCHOOL REPORT CARD	RATING
Net Cost After All Financial Aid	
Athletic Scholarship Offer	
Athletic Quality	
Academic Match	
Quality of Program	
Coaching Staff	
Coach's Interest Level in Me	
Potential for My Improvement	
Potential to Start in 1-2 Years	
Overall Impression	

COMMUNICATION RECORD

SCHOOL: ....

COACH	CONTACT INFO	MY INTEREST LEVEL (1-5)

DATE SENT INTRO PKT.	DATE COMPLETED QUESTIONNAIRE	DATE SENT VIDEO LINK	DATES SENT UPDATES

DATES	CONTACTS & NOTES

SCOUTING REPORT

Keep an ongoing scouting report on every school/program you are engaged with.
Consider: Athletics, Academics, Coaching Staff, Campus, Finances, and other priorities you have.

STRENGTHS:	WEAKNESSES:

SCHOOL REPORT CARD

SCHOOL REPORT CARD	RATING
Net Cost After All Financial Aid	
Athletic Scholarship Offer	
Athletic Quality	
Academic Match	
Quality of Program	
Coaching Staff	
Coach's Interest Level in Me	
Potential for My Improvement	
Potential to Start in 1-2 Years	
Overall Impression	

COMMUNICATION RECORD

SCHOOL: ....

COACH	CONTACT INFO	MY INTEREST LEVEL (1-5)

DATE SENT INTRO PKT.	DATE COMPLETED QUESTIONNAIRE	DATE SENT VIDEO LINK	DATES SENT UPDATES

DATES	CONTACTS & NOTES

SCOUTING REPORT

Keep an ongoing scouting report on every school/program you are engaged with.
Consider: Athletics, Academics, Coaching Staff, Campus, Finances, and other priorities you have.

STRENGTHS:	WEAKNESSES:

SCHOOL REPORT CARD

SCHOOL REPORT CARD	RATING
Net Cost After All Financial Aid	
Athletic Scholarship Offer	
Athletic Quality	
Academic Match	
Quality of Program	
Coaching Staff	
Coach's Interest Level in Me	
Potential for My Improvement	
Potential to Start in 1-2 Years	
Overall Impression	

COMMUNICATION RECORD

SCHOOL: _____

COACH	CONTACT INFO	MY INTEREST LEVEL (1-5)

DATE SENT INTRO PKT.	DATE COMPLETED QUESTIONNAIRE	DATE SENT VIDEO LINK	DATES SENT UPDATES

DATES	CONTACTS & NOTES

SCOUTING REPORT

Keep an ongoing scouting report on every school/program you are engaged with.
Consider: Athletics, Academics, Coaching Staff, Campus, Finances, and other priorities you have.

STRENGTHS:	WEAKNESSES:

SCHOOL REPORT CARD

SCHOOL REPORT CARD	RATING
Net Cost After All Financial Aid	
Athletic Scholarship Offer	
Athletic Quality	
Academic Match	
Quality of Program	
Coaching Staff	
Coach's Interest Level in Me	
Potential for My Improvement	
Potential to Start in 1-2 Years	
Overall Impression	

COMMUNICATION RECORD

SCHOOL:

COACH	CONTACT INFO	MY INTEREST LEVEL (1-5)

DATE SENT INTRO PKT.	DATE COMPLETED QUESTIONNAIRE	DATE SENT VIDEO LINK	DATES SENT UPDATES

DATES	CONTACTS & NOTES

SCOUTING REPORT

Keep an ongoing scouting report on every school/program you are engaged with.
Consider: Athletics, Academics, Coaching Staff, Campus, Finances, and other priorities you have.

STRENGTHS:	WEAKNESSES:

SCHOOL REPORT CARD

SCHOOL REPORT CARD	RATING
Net Cost After All Financial Aid	
Athletic Scholarship Offer	
Athletic Quality	
Academic Match	
Quality of Program	
Coaching Staff	
Coach's Interest Level in Me	
Potential for My Improvement	
Potential to Start in 1-2 Years	
Overall Impression	

COMMUNICATION RECORD

SCHOOL:

COACH	CONTACT INFO	MY INTEREST LEVEL (1-5)

DATE SENT INTRO PKT.	DATE COMPLETED QUESTIONNAIRE	DATE SENT VIDEO LINK	DATES SENT UPDATES

DATES	CONTACTS & NOTES

SCOUTING REPORT

Keep an ongoing scouting report on every school/program you are engaged with.
Consider: Athletics, Academics, Coaching Staff, Campus, Finances, and other priorities you have.

STRENGTHS:	WEAKNESSES:

SCHOOL REPORT CARD

SCHOOL REPORT CARD	RATING
Net Cost After All Financial Aid	
Athletic Scholarship Offer	
Athletic Quality	
Academic Match	
Quality of Program	
Coaching Staff	
Coach's Interest Level in Me	
Potential for My Improvement	
Potential to Start in 1-2 Years	
Overall Impression	

COMMUNICATION RECORD

SCHOOL:

COACH	CONTACT INFO	MY INTEREST LEVEL (1-5)

DATE SENT INTRO PKT.	DATE COMPLETED QUESTIONNAIRE	DATE SENT VIDEO LINK	DATES SENT UPDATES

DATES	CONTACTS & NOTES

SCOUTING REPORT

Keep an ongoing scouting report on every school/program you are engaged with.
Consider: Athletics, Academics, Coaching Staff, Campus, Finances, and other priorities you have.

STRENGTHS:	WEAKNESSES:

SCHOOL REPORT CARD

SCHOOL REPORT CARD	RATING
Net Cost After All Financial Aid	
Athletic Scholarship Offer	
Athletic Quality	
Academic Match	
Quality of Program	
Coaching Staff	
Coach's Interest Level in Me	
Potential for My Improvement	
Potential to Start in 1-2 Years	
Overall Impression	

COMMUNICATION RECORD

SCHOOL:

COACH	CONTACT INFO	MY INTEREST LEVEL (1-5)

DATE SENT INTRO PKT.	DATE COMPLETED QUESTIONNAIRE	DATE SENT VIDEO LINK	DATES SENT UPDATES

DATES	CONTACTS & NOTES

SCOUTING REPORT

Keep an ongoing scouting report on every school/program you are engaged with.
Consider: Athletics, Academics, Coaching Staff, Campus, Finances, and other priorities you have.

STRENGTHS:	WEAKNESSES:

SCHOOL REPORT CARD

SCHOOL REPORT CARD	RATING
Net Cost After All Financial Aid	
Athletic Scholarship Offer	
Athletic Quality	
Academic Match	
Quality of Program	
Coaching Staff	
Coach's Interest Level in Me	
Potential for My Improvement	
Potential to Start in 1-2 Years	
Overall Impression	

COMMUNICATION RECORD

SCHOOL: _____

COACH	CONTACT INFO	MY INTEREST LEVEL (1-5)

DATE SENT INTRO PKT.	DATE COMPLETED QUESTIONNAIRE	DATE SENT VIDEO LINK	DATES SENT UPDATES

DATES	CONTACTS & NOTES

SCOUTING REPORT

Keep an ongoing scouting report on every school/program you are engaged with.
Consider: Athletics, Academics, Coaching Staff, Campus, Finances, and other priorities you have.

STRENGTHS:	WEAKNESSES:

SCHOOL REPORT CARD

SCHOOL REPORT CARD	RATING
Net Cost After All Financial Aid	
Athletic Scholarship Offer	
Athletic Quality	
Academic Match	
Quality of Program	
Coaching Staff	
Coach's Interest Level in Me	
Potential for My Improvement	
Potential to Start in 1-2 Years	
Overall Impression	

COMMUNICATION RECORD

SCHOOL: _____

COACH	CONTACT INFO	MY INTEREST LEVEL (1-5)

DATE SENT INTRO PKT.	DATE COMPLETED QUESTIONNAIRE	DATE SENT VIDEO LINK	DATES SENT UPDATES

DATES	CONTACTS & NOTES

SCOUTING REPORT

Keep an ongoing scouting report on every school/program you are engaged with.
Consider: Athletics, Academics, Coaching Staff, Campus, Finances, and other priorities you have.

STRENGTHS:	WEAKNESSES:

SCHOOL REPORT CARD

SCHOOL REPORT CARD	RATING
Net Cost After All Financial Aid	
Athletic Scholarship Offer	
Athletic Quality	
Academic Match	
Quality of Program	
Coaching Staff	
Coach's Interest Level in Me	
Potential for My Improvement	
Potential to Start in 1-2 Years	
Overall Impression	

COMMUNICATION RECORD

SCHOOL: ....

COACH	CONTACT INFO	MY INTEREST LEVEL (1-5)

DATE SENT INTRO PKT.	DATE COMPLETED QUESTIONNAIRE	DATE SENT VIDEO LINK	DATES SENT UPDATES

DATES	CONTACTS & NOTES

SCOUTING REPORT

Keep an ongoing scouting report on every school/program you are engaged with.
Consider: Athletics, Academics, Coaching Staff, Campus, Finances, and other priorities you have.

STRENGTHS:	WEAKNESSES:

SCHOOL REPORT CARD

SCHOOL REPORT CARD	RATING
Net Cost After All Financial Aid	
Athletic Scholarship Offer	
Athletic Quality	
Academic Match	
Quality of Program	
Coaching Staff	
Coach's Interest Level in Me	
Potential for My Improvement	
Potential to Start in 1-2 Years	
Overall Impression	

COMMUNICATION RECORD

SCHOOL:

COACH	CONTACT INFO	MY INTEREST LEVEL (1-5)

DATE SENT INTRO PKT.	DATE COMPLETED QUESTIONNAIRE	DATE SENT VIDEO LINK	DATES SENT UPDATES

DATES	CONTACTS & NOTES

SCOUTING REPORT

Keep an ongoing scouting report on every school/program you are engaged with.
Consider: Athletics, Academics, Coaching Staff, Campus, Finances, and other priorities you have.

STRENGTHS:	WEAKNESSES:

SCHOOL REPORT CARD

SCHOOL REPORT CARD	RATING
Net Cost After All Financial Aid	
Athletic Scholarship Offer	
Athletic Quality	
Academic Match	
Quality of Program	
Coaching Staff	
Coach's Interest Level in Me	
Potential for My Improvement	
Potential to Start in 1-2 Years	
Overall Impression	

COMMUNICATION RECORD

SCHOOL: ....

COACH	CONTACT INFO	MY INTEREST LEVEL (1-5)

DATE SENT INTRO PKT.	DATE COMPLETED QUESTIONNAIRE	DATE SENT VIDEO LINK	DATES SENT UPDATES

DATES	CONTACTS & NOTES

SCOUTING REPORT

Keep an ongoing scouting report on every school/program you are engaged with.
Consider: Athletics, Academics, Coaching Staff, Campus, Finances, and other priorities you have.

STRENGTHS:	WEAKNESSES:

SCHOOL REPORT CARD

SCHOOL REPORT CARD	RATING
Net Cost After All Financial Aid	
Athletic Scholarship Offer	
Athletic Quality	
Academic Match	
Quality of Program	
Coaching Staff	
Coach's Interest Level in Me	
Potential for My Improvement	
Potential to Start in 1-2 Years	
Overall Impression	

COMMUNICATION RECORD

SCHOOL:

COACH	CONTACT INFO	MY INTEREST LEVEL (1-5)

DATE SENT INTRO PKT.	DATE COMPLETED QUESTIONNAIRE	DATE SENT VIDEO LINK	DATES SENT UPDATES

DATES	CONTACTS & NOTES

SCOUTING REPORT

Keep an ongoing scouting report on every school/program you are engaged with.
Consider: Athletics, Academics, Coaching Staff, Campus, Finances, and other priorities you have.

STRENGTHS:	WEAKNESSES:

SCHOOL REPORT CARD

SCHOOL REPORT CARD	RATING
Net Cost After All Financial Aid	
Athletic Scholarship Offer	
Athletic Quality	
Academic Match	
Quality of Program	
Coaching Staff	
Coach's Interest Level in Me	
Potential for My Improvement	
Potential to Start in 1-2 Years	
Overall Impression	

COMMUNICATION RECORD

SCHOOL: ....

COACH	CONTACT INFO	MY INTEREST LEVEL (1-5)

DATE SENT INTRO PKT.	DATE COMPLETED QUESTIONNAIRE	DATE SENT VIDEO LINK	DATES SENT UPDATES

DATES	CONTACTS & NOTES

SCOUTING REPORT

Keep an ongoing scouting report on every school/program you are engaged with.
Consider: Athletics, Academics, Coaching Staff, Campus, Finances, and other priorities you have.

STRENGTHS:	WEAKNESSES:

SCHOOL REPORT CARD

SCHOOL REPORT CARD	RATING
Net Cost After All Financial Aid	
Athletic Scholarship Offer	
Athletic Quality	
Academic Match	
Quality of Program	
Coaching Staff	
Coach's Interest Level in Me	
Potential for My Improvement	
Potential to Start in 1-2 Years	
Overall Impression	

COMMUNICATION RECORD

SCHOOL:

COACH	CONTACT INFO	MY INTEREST LEVEL (1-5)

DATE SENT INTRO PKT.	DATE COMPLETED QUESTIONNAIRE	DATE SENT VIDEO LINK	DATES SENT UPDATES

DATES	CONTACTS & NOTES

SCOUTING REPORT

Keep an ongoing scouting report on every school/program you are engaged with.
Consider: Athletics, Academics, Coaching Staff, Campus, Finances, and other priorities you have.

STRENGTHS:	WEAKNESSES:

SCHOOL REPORT CARD

SCHOOL REPORT CARD	RATING
Net Cost After All Financial Aid	
Athletic Scholarship Offer	
Athletic Quality	
Academic Match	
Quality of Program	
Coaching Staff	
Coach's Interest Level in Me	
Potential for My Improvement	
Potential to Start in 1-2 Years	
Overall Impression	

COMMUNICATION RECORD

SCHOOL: _____

COACH	CONTACT INFO	MY INTEREST LEVEL (1-5)

DATE SENT INTRO PKT.	DATE COMPLETED QUESTIONNAIRE	DATE SENT VIDEO LINK	DATES SENT UPDATES

DATES	CONTACTS & NOTES

SCOUTING REPORT

Keep an ongoing scouting report on every school/program you are engaged with.
Consider: Athletics, Academics, Coaching Staff, Campus, Finances, and other priorities you have.

STRENGTHS:	WEAKNESSES:

SCHOOL REPORT CARD

SCHOOL REPORT CARD	RATING
Net Cost After All Financial Aid	
Athletic Scholarship Offer	
Athletic Quality	
Academic Match	
Quality of Program	
Coaching Staff	
Coach's Interest Level in Me	
Potential for My Improvement	
Potential to Start in 1-2 Years	
Overall Impression	

COMMUNICATION RECORD

SCHOOL:

COACH	CONTACT INFO	MY INTEREST LEVEL (1-5)

DATE SENT INTRO PKT.	DATE COMPLETED QUESTIONNAIRE	DATE SENT VIDEO LINK	DATES SENT UPDATES

DATES	CONTACTS & NOTES

SCOUTING REPORT

Keep an ongoing scouting report on every school/program you are engaged with.
Consider: Athletics, Academics, Coaching Staff, Campus, Finances, and other priorities you have.

STRENGTHS:	WEAKNESSES:

SCHOOL REPORT CARD

SCHOOL REPORT CARD	RATING
Net Cost After All Financial Aid	
Athletic Scholarship Offer	
Athletic Quality	
Academic Match	
Quality of Program	
Coaching Staff	
Coach's Interest Level in Me	
Potential for My Improvement	
Potential to Start in 1-2 Years	
Overall Impression	

COMMUNICATION RECORD

SCHOOL: ....

COACH	CONTACT INFO	MY INTEREST LEVEL (1-5)

DATE SENT INTRO PKT.	DATE COMPLETED QUESTIONNAIRE	DATE SENT VIDEO LINK	DATES SENT UPDATES

DATES	CONTACTS & NOTES

SCOUTING REPORT

Keep an ongoing scouting report on every school/program you are engaged with.
Consider: Athletics, Academics, Coaching Staff, Campus, Finances, and other priorities you have.

STRENGTHS:	WEAKNESSES:

SCHOOL REPORT CARD

SCHOOL REPORT CARD	RATING
Net Cost After All Financial Aid	
Athletic Scholarship Offer	
Athletic Quality	
Academic Match	
Quality of Program	
Coaching Staff	
Coach's Interest Level in Me	
Potential for My Improvement	
Potential to Start in 1-2 Years	
Overall Impression	

COMMUNICATION RECORD

SCHOOL: ....

COACH	CONTACT INFO	MY INTEREST LEVEL (1-5)

DATE SENT INTRO PKT.	DATE COMPLETED QUESTIONNAIRE	DATE SENT VIDEO LINK	DATES SENT UPDATES

DATES	CONTACTS & NOTES

SCOUTING REPORT

Keep an ongoing scouting report on every school/program you are engaged with.
Consider: Athletics, Academics, Coaching Staff, Campus, Finances, and other priorities you have.

STRENGTHS:	WEAKNESSES:

SCHOOL REPORT CARD

SCHOOL REPORT CARD	RATING
Net Cost After All Financial Aid	
Athletic Scholarship Offer	
Athletic Quality	
Academic Match	
Quality of Program	
Coaching Staff	
Coach's Interest Level in Me	
Potential for My Improvement	
Potential to Start in 1-2 Years	
Overall Impression	

COMMUNICATION RECORD

SCHOOL:

COACH	CONTACT INFO	MY INTEREST LEVEL (1-5)

DATE SENT INTRO PKT.	DATE COMPLETED QUESTIONNAIRE	DATE SENT VIDEO LINK	DATES SENT UPDATES

DATES	CONTACTS & NOTES

SCOUTING REPORT

Keep an ongoing scouting report on every school/program you are engaged with.
Consider: Athletics, Academics, Coaching Staff, Campus, Finances, and other priorities you have.

STRENGTHS:	WEAKNESSES:

SCHOOL REPORT CARD

SCHOOL REPORT CARD	RATING
Net Cost After All Financial Aid	
Athletic Scholarship Offer	
Athletic Quality	
Academic Match	
Quality of Program	
Coaching Staff	
Coach's Interest Level in Me	
Potential for My Improvement	
Potential to Start in 1-2 Years	
Overall Impression	

COMMUNICATION RECORD

SCHOOL: _____

COACH	CONTACT INFO	MY INTEREST LEVEL (1-5)

DATE SENT INTRO PKT.	DATE COMPLETED QUESTIONNAIRE	DATE SENT VIDEO LINK	DATES SENT UPDATES

DATES	CONTACTS & NOTES

SCOUTING REPORT

Keep an ongoing scouting report on every school/program you are engaged with.
Consider: Athletics, Academics, Coaching Staff, Campus, Finances, and other priorities you have.

STRENGTHS:	WEAKNESSES:

SCHOOL REPORT CARD

SCHOOL REPORT CARD	RATING
Net Cost After All Financial Aid	
Athletic Scholarship Offer	
Athletic Quality	
Academic Match	
Quality of Program	
Coaching Staff	
Coach's Interest Level in Me	
Potential for My Improvement	
Potential to Start in 1-2 Years	
Overall Impression	

COMMUNICATION RECORD

SCHOOL: ....

COACH	CONTACT INFO	MY INTEREST LEVEL (1-5)

DATE SENT INTRO PKT.	DATE COMPLETED QUESTIONNAIRE	DATE SENT VIDEO LINK	DATES SENT UPDATES

DATES	CONTACTS & NOTES

SCOUTING REPORT

Keep an ongoing scouting report on every school/program you are engaged with.
Consider: Athletics, Academics, Coaching Staff, Campus, Finances, and other priorities you have.

STRENGTHS:	WEAKNESSES:

SCHOOL REPORT CARD

SCHOOL REPORT CARD	RATING
Net Cost After All Financial Aid	
Athletic Scholarship Offer	
Athletic Quality	
Academic Match	
Quality of Program	
Coaching Staff	
Coach's Interest Level in Me	
Potential for My Improvement	
Potential to Start in 1-2 Years	
Overall Impression	

COMMUNICATION RECORD

SCHOOL: ....

COACH	CONTACT INFO	MY INTEREST LEVEL (1-5)

DATE SENT INTRO PKT.	DATE COMPLETED QUESTIONNAIRE	DATE SENT VIDEO LINK	DATES SENT UPDATES

DATES	CONTACTS & NOTES

SCOUTING REPORT

Keep an ongoing scouting report on every school/program you are engaged with.
Consider: Athletics, Academics, Coaching Staff, Campus, Finances, and other priorities you have.

STRENGTHS:	WEAKNESSES:

SCHOOL REPORT CARD

SCHOOL REPORT CARD	RATING
Net Cost After All Financial Aid	
Athletic Scholarship Offer	
Athletic Quality	
Academic Match	
Quality of Program	
Coaching Staff	
Coach's Interest Level in Me	
Potential for My Improvement	
Potential to Start in 1-2 Years	
Overall Impression	

COMMUNICATION RECORD

SCHOOL: _____

COACH	CONTACT INFO	MY INTEREST LEVEL (1-5)

DATE SENT INTRO PKT.	DATE COMPLETED QUESTIONNAIRE	DATE SENT VIDEO LINK	DATES SENT UPDATES

DATES	CONTACTS & NOTES

SCOUTING REPORT

Keep an ongoing scouting report on every school/program you are engaged with.
Consider: Athletics, Academics, Coaching Staff, Campus, Finances, and other priorities you have.

STRENGTHS:	WEAKNESSES:

SCHOOL REPORT CARD

SCHOOL REPORT CARD	RATING
Net Cost After All Financial Aid	
Athletic Scholarship Offer	
Athletic Quality	
Academic Match	
Quality of Program	
Coaching Staff	
Coach's Interest Level in Me	
Potential for My Improvement	
Potential to Start in 1-2 Years	
Overall Impression	

COMMUNICATION RECORD

SCHOOL: ....

COACH	CONTACT INFO	MY INTEREST LEVEL (1-5)

DATE SENT INTRO PKT.	DATE COMPLETED QUESTIONNAIRE	DATE SENT VIDEO LINK	DATES SENT UPDATES

DATES	CONTACTS & NOTES

SCOUTING REPORT

Keep an ongoing scouting report on every school/program you are engaged with.
Consider: Athletics, Academics, Coaching Staff, Campus, Finances, and other priorities you have.

STRENGTHS:	WEAKNESSES:

SCHOOL REPORT CARD

SCHOOL REPORT CARD	RATING
Net Cost After All Financial Aid	
Athletic Scholarship Offer	
Athletic Quality	
Academic Match	
Quality of Program	
Coaching Staff	
Coach's Interest Level in Me	
Potential for My Improvement	
Potential to Start in 1-2 Years	
Overall Impression	

COMMUNICATION RECORD

SCHOOL:

COACH	CONTACT INFO	MY INTEREST LEVEL (1-5)

DATE SENT INTRO PKT.	DATE COMPLETED QUESTIONNAIRE	DATE SENT VIDEO LINK	DATES SENT UPDATES

DATES	CONTACTS & NOTES

SCOUTING REPORT

Keep an ongoing scouting report on every school/program you are engaged with.
Consider: Athletics, Academics, Coaching Staff, Campus, Finances, and other priorities you have.

STRENGTHS:	WEAKNESSES:

SCHOOL REPORT CARD

SCHOOL REPORT CARD	RATING
Net Cost After All Financial Aid	
Athletic Scholarship Offer	
Athletic Quality	
Academic Match	
Quality of Program	
Coaching Staff	
Coach's Interest Level in Me	
Potential for My Improvement	
Potential to Start in 1-2 Years	
Overall Impression	

COMMUNICATION RECORD

SCHOOL: ....

COACH	CONTACT INFO	MY INTEREST LEVEL (1-5)

DATE SENT INTRO PKT.	DATE COMPLETED QUESTIONNAIRE	DATE SENT VIDEO LINK	DATES SENT UPDATES

DATES	CONTACTS & NOTES

SCOUTING REPORT

Keep an ongoing scouting report on every school/program you are engaged with.
Consider: Athletics, Academics, Coaching Staff, Campus, Finances, and other priorities you have.

STRENGTHS:	WEAKNESSES:

SCHOOL REPORT CARD

SCHOOL REPORT CARD	RATING
Net Cost After All Financial Aid	
Athletic Scholarship Offer	
Athletic Quality	
Academic Match	
Quality of Program	
Coaching Staff	
Coach's Interest Level in Me	
Potential for My Improvement	
Potential to Start in 1-2 Years	
Overall Impression	

COMMUNICATION RECORD

SCHOOL: ....

COACH	CONTACT INFO	MY INTEREST LEVEL (1-5)

DATE SENT INTRO PKT.	DATE COMPLETED QUESTIONNAIRE	DATE SENT VIDEO LINK	DATES SENT UPDATES

DATES	CONTACTS & NOTES

SCOUTING REPORT

Keep an ongoing scouting report on every school/program you are engaged with.
Consider: Athletics, Academics, Coaching Staff, Campus, Finances, and other priorities you have.

STRENGTHS:	WEAKNESSES:

SCHOOL REPORT CARD

SCHOOL REPORT CARD	RATING
Net Cost After All Financial Aid	
Athletic Scholarship Offer	
Athletic Quality	
Academic Match	
Quality of Program	
Coaching Staff	
Coach's Interest Level in Me	
Potential for My Improvement	
Potential to Start in 1-2 Years	
Overall Impression	

COMMUNICATION RECORD

SCHOOL:

COACH	CONTACT INFO	MY INTEREST LEVEL (1-5)

DATE SENT INTRO PKT.	DATE COMPLETED QUESTIONNAIRE	DATE SENT VIDEO LINK	DATES SENT UPDATES

DATES	CONTACTS & NOTES

SCOUTING REPORT

Keep an ongoing scouting report on every school/program you are engaged with.
Consider: Athletics, Academics, Coaching Staff, Campus, Finances, and other priorities you have.

STRENGTHS:	WEAKNESSES:

SCHOOL REPORT CARD

SCHOOL REPORT CARD	RATING
Net Cost After All Financial Aid	
Athletic Scholarship Offer	
Athletic Quality	
Academic Match	
Quality of Program	
Coaching Staff	
Coach's Interest Level in Me	
Potential for My Improvement	
Potential to Start in 1-2 Years	
Overall Impression	

COMMUNICATION RECORD

SCHOOL: ....

COACH	CONTACT INFO	MY INTEREST LEVEL (1-5)

DATE SENT INTRO PKT.	DATE COMPLETED QUESTIONNAIRE	DATE SENT VIDEO LINK	DATES SENT UPDATES

DATES	CONTACTS & NOTES

SCOUTING REPORT

Keep an ongoing scouting report on every school/program you are engaged with.
Consider: Athletics, Academics, Coaching Staff, Campus, Finances, and other priorities you have.

STRENGTHS:	WEAKNESSES:

SCHOOL REPORT CARD

SCHOOL REPORT CARD	RATING
Net Cost After All Financial Aid	
Athletic Scholarship Offer	
Athletic Quality	
Academic Match	
Quality of Program	
Coaching Staff	
Coach's Interest Level in Me	
Potential for My Improvement	
Potential to Start in 1-2 Years	
Overall Impression	

COMMUNICATION RECORD

SCHOOL:

COACH	CONTACT INFO	MY INTEREST LEVEL (1-5)

DATE SENT INTRO PKT.	DATE COMPLETED QUESTIONNAIRE	DATE SENT VIDEO LINK	DATES SENT UPDATES

DATES	CONTACTS & NOTES

SCOUTING REPORT

Keep an ongoing scouting report on every school/program you are engaged with.
Consider: Athletics, Academics, Coaching Staff, Campus, Finances, and other priorities you have.

STRENGTHS:	WEAKNESSES:

SCHOOL REPORT CARD

SCHOOL REPORT CARD	RATING
Net Cost After All Financial Aid	
Athletic Scholarship Offer	
Athletic Quality	
Academic Match	
Quality of Program	
Coaching Staff	
Coach's Interest Level in Me	
Potential for My Improvement	
Potential to Start in 1-2 Years	
Overall Impression	

COMMUNICATION RECORD

SCHOOL: ....

COACH	CONTACT INFO	MY INTEREST LEVEL (1-5)

DATE SENT INTRO PKT.	DATE COMPLETED QUESTIONNAIRE	DATE SENT VIDEO LINK	DATES SENT UPDATES

DATES	CONTACTS & NOTES

SCOUTING REPORT

Keep an ongoing scouting report on every school/program you are engaged with.
Consider: Athletics, Academics, Coaching Staff, Campus, Finances, and other priorities you have.

STRENGTHS:	WEAKNESSES:

SCHOOL REPORT CARD

SCHOOL REPORT CARD	RATING
Net Cost After All Financial Aid	
Athletic Scholarship Offer	
Athletic Quality	
Academic Match	
Quality of Program	
Coaching Staff	
Coach's Interest Level in Me	
Potential for My Improvement	
Potential to Start in 1-2 Years	
Overall Impression	

COMMUNICATION RECORD

SCHOOL:

COACH	CONTACT INFO	MY INTEREST LEVEL (1-5)

DATE SENT INTRO PKT.	DATE COMPLETED QUESTIONNAIRE	DATE SENT VIDEO LINK	DATES SENT UPDATES

DATES	CONTACTS & NOTES

SCOUTING REPORT

Keep an ongoing scouting report on every school/program you are engaged with.
Consider: Athletics, Academics, Coaching Staff, Campus, Finances, and other priorities you have.

STRENGTHS:	WEAKNESSES:

SCHOOL REPORT CARD

SCHOOL REPORT CARD	RATING
Net Cost After All Financial Aid	
Athletic Scholarship Offer	
Athletic Quality	
Academic Match	
Quality of Program	
Coaching Staff	
Coach's Interest Level in Me	
Potential for My Improvement	
Potential to Start in 1-2 Years	
Overall Impression	

COMMUNICATION RECORD

SCHOOL:

COACH	CONTACT INFO	MY INTEREST LEVEL (1-5)

DATE SENT INTRO PKT.	DATE COMPLETED QUESTIONNAIRE	DATE SENT VIDEO LINK	DATES SENT UPDATES

DATES	CONTACTS & NOTES

SCOUTING REPORT

Keep an ongoing scouting report on every school/program you are engaged with.
Consider: Athletics, Academics, Coaching Staff, Campus, Finances, and other priorities you have.

STRENGTHS:	WEAKNESSES:

SCHOOL REPORT CARD

SCHOOL REPORT CARD	RATING
Net Cost After All Financial Aid	
Athletic Scholarship Offer	
Athletic Quality	
Academic Match	
Quality of Program	
Coaching Staff	
Coach's Interest Level in Me	
Potential for My Improvement	
Potential to Start in 1-2 Years	
Overall Impression	

COMMUNICATION RECORD

SCHOOL:

COACH	CONTACT INFO	MY INTEREST LEVEL (1-5)

DATE SENT INTRO PKT.	DATE COMPLETED QUESTIONNAIRE	DATE SENT VIDEO LINK	DATES SENT UPDATES

DATES	CONTACTS & NOTES

SCOUTING REPORT

Keep an ongoing scouting report on every school/program you are engaged with.
Consider: Athletics, Academics, Coaching Staff, Campus, Finances, and other priorities you have.

STRENGTHS:	WEAKNESSES:

SCHOOL REPORT CARD

SCHOOL REPORT CARD	RATING
Net Cost After All Financial Aid	
Athletic Scholarship Offer	
Athletic Quality	
Academic Match	
Quality of Program	
Coaching Staff	
Coach's Interest Level in Me	
Potential for My Improvement	
Potential to Start in 1-2 Years	
Overall Impression	

COMMUNICATION RECORD

SCHOOL: ....

COACH	CONTACT INFO	MY INTEREST LEVEL (1-5)

DATE SENT INTRO PKT.	DATE COMPLETED QUESTIONNAIRE	DATE SENT VIDEO LINK	DATES SENT UPDATES

DATES	CONTACTS & NOTES

SCOUTING REPORT

Keep an ongoing scouting report on every school/program you are engaged with.
Consider: Athletics, Academics, Coaching Staff, Campus, Finances, and other priorities you have.

STRENGTHS:	WEAKNESSES:

SCHOOL REPORT CARD

SCHOOL REPORT CARD	RATING
Net Cost After All Financial Aid	
Athletic Scholarship Offer	
Athletic Quality	
Academic Match	
Quality of Program	
Coaching Staff	
Coach's Interest Level in Me	
Potential for My Improvement	
Potential to Start in 1-2 Years	
Overall Impression	

COMMUNICATION RECORD

SCHOOL: ....

COACH	CONTACT INFO	MY INTEREST LEVEL (1-5)

DATE SENT INTRO PKT.	DATE COMPLETED QUESTIONNAIRE	DATE SENT VIDEO LINK	DATES SENT UPDATES

DATES	CONTACTS & NOTES

SCOUTING REPORT

Keep an ongoing scouting report on every school/program you are engaged with.
Consider: Athletics, Academics, Coaching Staff, Campus, Finances, and other priorities you have.

STRENGTHS:	WEAKNESSES:

SCHOOL REPORT CARD

SCHOOL REPORT CARD	RATING
Net Cost After All Financial Aid	
Athletic Scholarship Offer	
Athletic Quality	
Academic Match	
Quality of Program	
Coaching Staff	
Coach's Interest Level in Me	
Potential for My Improvement	
Potential to Start in 1-2 Years	
Overall Impression	

COMMUNICATION RECORD

SCHOOL: _____

COACH	CONTACT INFO	MY INTEREST LEVEL (1-5)

DATE SENT INTRO PKT.	DATE COMPLETED QUESTIONNAIRE	DATE SENT VIDEO LINK	DATES SENT UPDATES

DATES	CONTACTS & NOTES

SCOUTING REPORT

Keep an ongoing scouting report on every school/program you are engaged with.
Consider: Athletics, Academics, Coaching Staff, Campus, Finances, and other priorities you have.

STRENGTHS:	WEAKNESSES:

SCHOOL REPORT CARD

SCHOOL REPORT CARD	RATING
Net Cost After All Financial Aid	
Athletic Scholarship Offer	
Athletic Quality	
Academic Match	
Quality of Program	
Coaching Staff	
Coach's Interest Level in Me	
Potential for My Improvement	
Potential to Start in 1-2 Years	
Overall Impression	

COMMUNICATION RECORD

SCHOOL:

COACH	CONTACT INFO	MY INTEREST LEVEL (1-5)

DATE SENT INTRO PKT.	DATE COMPLETED QUESTIONNAIRE	DATE SENT VIDEO LINK	DATES SENT UPDATES

DATES	CONTACTS & NOTES

SCOUTING REPORT

Keep an ongoing scouting report on every school/program you are engaged with.
Consider: Athletics, Academics, Coaching Staff, Campus, Finances, and other priorities you have.

STRENGTHS:	WEAKNESSES:

SCHOOL REPORT CARD

SCHOOL REPORT CARD	RATING
Net Cost After All Financial Aid	
Athletic Scholarship Offer	
Athletic Quality	
Academic Match	
Quality of Program	
Coaching Staff	
Coach's Interest Level in Me	
Potential for My Improvement	
Potential to Start in 1-2 Years	
Overall Impression	

COMMUNICATION RECORD

SCHOOL: ....

COACH	CONTACT INFO	MY INTEREST LEVEL (1-5)

DATE SENT INTRO PKT.	DATE COMPLETED QUESTIONNAIRE	DATE SENT VIDEO LINK	DATES SENT UPDATES

DATES	CONTACTS & NOTES

SCOUTING REPORT

Keep an ongoing scouting report on every school/program you are engaged with.
Consider: Athletics, Academics, Coaching Staff, Campus, Finances, and other priorities you have.

STRENGTHS:	WEAKNESSES:

SCHOOL REPORT CARD

SCHOOL REPORT CARD	RATING
Net Cost After All Financial Aid	
Athletic Scholarship Offer	
Athletic Quality	
Academic Match	
Quality of Program	
Coaching Staff	
Coach's Interest Level in Me	
Potential for My Improvement	
Potential to Start in 1-2 Years	
Overall Impression	

CAMPUS VISIT NOTES

Complete top section before your visit.

School: FORDHAM

Coach(es): Bill Williams

Admissions Contact: Ellen Warrington

Date of Visit: 7/21

Appointment Time(s): 9:00am Admissions 11:00am Coach

Appointment Location(s): #1 – Admissions Office

#2 – Field House – Take campus bus #7

Visit Notes (impressions, what I/we did, best points, worst points):

The admissions staff were very helpful. They helped us understand what it really takes to get admitted, what deadlines are coming, and best time to apply.

The campus didn't feel right. Not sure why. People weren't that friendly.

Coach Williams was great. He leveled with us about my chances. He is also looking at another kid for my position. He will know more in 2 weeks. We didn't talk about $$.

Follow-Up Actions to be Taken:

☐ Check back w/ Coach on 8/10

☐ Read through class descriptions in my major

☐ Decide by 9/15 if I will apply

CAMPUS VISIT NOTES

Complete top section before your visit.

School: ....

Coach(es): ....

Admissions Contact: ....

Date of Visit: .... **Appointment Time(s):** ....

Appointment Location(s): ....

....

Visit Notes (impressions, what I/we did, best points, worst points):

....

....

....

....

....

....

....

....

....

Follow-Up Actions to be Taken:

❏ ....

❏ ....

❏ ....

CAMPUS VISIT NOTES

Complete top section before your visit.

School: ....

Coach(es): ....

Admissions Contact: ....

Date of Visit: .... **Appointment Time(s):** ....

Appointment Location(s): ....

....

Visit Notes (impressions, what I/we did, best points, worst points):

....

....

....

....

....

....

....

....

....

....

Follow-Up Actions to be Taken:

❑ ....

❑ ....

❑ ....

CAMPUS VISIT NOTES

Complete top section before your visit.

School:

Coach(es):

Admissions Contact:

Date of Visit: **Appointment Time(s):**

Appointment Location(s):

Visit Notes (impressions, what I/we did, best points, worst points):

Follow-Up Actions to be Taken:

❏

❏

❏

CAMPUS VISIT NOTES

Complete top section before your visit.

School:

Coach(es):

Admissions Contact:

Date of Visit: **Appointment Time(s):**

Appointment Location(s):

Visit Notes (impressions, what I/we did, best points, worst points):

Follow-Up Actions to be Taken:

❑

❑

❑

CAMPUS VISIT NOTES

Complete top section before your visit.

School: ....

Coach(es): ....

Admissions Contact: ....

Date of Visit: .... **Appointment Time(s):** ....

Appointment Location(s): ....

Visit Notes (impressions, what I/we did, best points, worst points):

....

....

....

....

....

....

....

....

....

Follow-Up Actions to be Taken:

❏ ....

❏ ....

❏ ....

CAMPUS VISIT NOTES

Complete top section before your visit.

School: ....

Coach(es): ....

Admissions Contact: ....

Date of Visit: .... **Appointment Time(s):** ....

Appointment Location(s): ....

....

Visit Notes (impressions, what I/we did, best points, worst points):

....

....

....

....

....

....

....

....

....

....

....

Follow-Up Actions to be Taken:

❏ ....

❏ ....

❏ ....

CAMPUS VISIT NOTES

Complete top section before your visit.

School:

Coach(es):

Admissions Contact:

Date of Visit: **Appointment Time(s):**

Appointment Location(s):

Visit Notes (impressions, what I/we did, best points, worst points):

Follow-Up Actions to be Taken:

❑

❑

❑

CAMPUS VISIT NOTES

Complete top section before your visit.

School: _____

Coach(es): _____

Admissions Contact: _____

Date of Visit: _____ **Appointment Time(s):** _____

Appointment Location(s): _____

_____

Visit Notes (impressions, what I/we did, best points, worst points):

_____

_____

_____

_____

_____

_____

_____

_____

_____

_____

_____

_____

Follow-Up Actions to be Taken:

❑ _____

❑ _____

❑ _____

CAMPUS VISIT NOTES

Complete top section before your visit.

School: ....

Coach(es): ....

Admissions Contact: ....

Date of Visit: .... **Appointment Time(s):** ....

Appointment Location(s): ....

....

Visit Notes (impressions, what I/we did, best points, worst points):

....

....

....

....

....

....

....

....

....

Follow-Up Actions to be Taken:

❏ ....

❏ ....

❏ ....

CAMPUS VISIT NOTES

Complete top section before your visit.

School:

Coach(es):

Admissions Contact:

Date of Visit: **Appointment Time(s):**

Appointment Location(s):

Visit Notes (impressions, what I/we did, best points, worst points):

Follow-Up Actions to be Taken:

❑

❑

❑

CAMPUS VISIT NOTES

Complete top section before your visit.

School:

Coach(es):

Admissions Contact:

Date of Visit: **Appointment Time(s):**

Appointment Location(s):

Visit Notes (impressions, what I/we did, best points, worst points):

Follow-Up Actions to be Taken:

❑

❑

❑

CAMPUS VISIT NOTES

Complete top section before your visit.

School:

Coach(es):

Admissions Contact:

Date of Visit: **Appointment Time(s):**

Appointment Location(s):

Visit Notes (impressions, what I/we did, best points, worst points):

Follow-Up Actions to be Taken:

❑

❑

❑

CAMPUS VISIT NOTES

Complete top section before your visit.

School:

Coach(es):

Admissions Contact:

Date of Visit: **Appointment Time(s):**

Appointment Location(s):

Visit Notes (impressions, what I/we did, best points, worst points):

Follow-Up Actions to be Taken:

❏

❏

❏

CAMPUS VISIT NOTES

Complete top section before your visit.

School:

Coach(es):

Admissions Contact:

Date of Visit: **Appointment Time(s):**

Appointment Location(s):

Visit Notes (impressions, what I/we did, best points, worst points):

Follow-Up Actions to be Taken:

❏

❏

❏

CAMPUS VISIT NOTES

Complete top section before your visit.

School: ....

Coach(es): ....

Admissions Contact: ....

Date of Visit: .... **Appointment Time(s):** ....

Appointment Location(s): ....

....

Visit Notes (impressions, what I/we did, best points, worst points):

....

....

....

....

....

....

....

....

....

Follow-Up Actions to be Taken:

❑ ....

❑ ....

❑ ....

CAMPUS VISIT NOTES

Complete top section before your visit.

School:

Coach(es):

Admissions Contact:

Date of Visit: **Appointment Time(s):**

Appointment Location(s):

Visit Notes (impressions, what I/we did, best points, worst points):

Follow-Up Actions to be Taken:

❏

❏

❏

CAMPUS VISIT NOTES

Complete top section before your visit.

School: ....

Coach(es): ....

Admissions Contact: ....

Date of Visit: .... **Appointment Time(s):** ....

Appointment Location(s): ....

....

Visit Notes (impressions, what I/we did, best points, worst points):

....

....

....

....

....

....

....

....

Follow-Up Actions to be Taken:

❏ ....

❏ ....

❏ ....

CAMPUS VISIT NOTES

Complete top section before your visit.

School: ....

Coach(es): ....

Admissions Contact: ....

Date of Visit: .... **Appointment Time(s):** ....

Appointment Location(s): ....

....

Visit Notes (impressions, what I/we did, best points, worst points):

....

....

....

....

....

....

....

....

....

Follow-Up Actions to be Taken:

❏ ....

❏ ....

❏ ....

CAMPUS VISIT NOTES

Complete top section before your visit.

School:

Coach(es):

Admissions Contact:

Date of Visit: **Appointment Time(s):**

Appointment Location(s):

Visit Notes (impressions, what I/we did, best points, worst points):

Follow-Up Actions to be Taken:

❑

❑

❑

COMPARATIVE SCHOOL REPORT CARDS

Making your final school choice can be difficult. However, if you've created Report Cards on each one, your decision will be easier. You have already created a Report Card for each of your prospective schools earlier in the Planner. As you get closer to making your decision, include the Report Cards of up to 12 top prospective schools. When you put them side-by-side on the following page, the picture will be more clear.

SCHOOL LIST FOR REPORT CARDS

1. ....
2. ....
3. ....
4. ....
5. ....
6. ....

7. ....
8. ....
9. ....
10. ....
11. ....
12. ....

	SCHOOL RATING					
School # in List →	1	2	3	4	5	6
Net Cost After All Financial Aid	12,000	21,000	15,000	41,000	20,000	17,500
Athletic Scholarship Offer	15,000	8,000	13,000	2,000	15,000	12,000
Athletic Quality	A-	C	B	B+	C	A
Academic Match	A	A	B	C	C	B
Quality of Program	A	B-	B-	B-	D	B+
Coaching Staff	A	A	A	B	C	C
Coach's Interest Level in Me	A	B	B	A	B	C
Potential for My Improvement	B+	B+	A	C	A-	B-
Potential to Start in 1–2 Years	A	A	A	B	A	B
Overall Impression	A	B	B	B+	B-	C
School size for my desires	A	B-	B-	B	B	B-

SCHOOL RATING						
School # in List →	1	2	3	4	5	6
Net Cost After All Financial Aid						
Athletic Scholarship Offer						
Athletic Quality						
Academic Match						
Quality of Program						
Coaching Staff						
Coach's Interest Level in Me						
Potential for My Improvement						
Potential to Start in 1-2 Years						
Overall Impression						

SCHOOL RATING						
School # in List →	7	8	9	10	11	12
Net Cost After All Financial Aid						
Athletic Scholarship Offer						
Athletic Quality						
Academic Match						
Quality of Program						
Coaching Staff						
Coach's Interest Level in Me						
Potential for My Improvement						
Potential to Start in 1-2 Years						
Overall Impression						

COMPARATIVE REPORTS

ABOUT THE AUTHOR

JON FUGLER is a recruiting expert, author, and CEO of Recruit-Me. He has been coaching families through the athletic scholarship process since 2002. It all started when his twin sons were seeking athletic scholarships a few years earlier.

With a daughter already in college, Jon and his wife knew that they needed financial help. Their sons were talented athletes, so the family received counsel and coaching from a seasoned expert. Both boys landed fully-paid educations at the school of their choice.

Soon after, Jon co-founded *Recruit-Me*, and since then he has helped thousands of families navigate the recruiting process. Jon has spoken to parent and athlete groups, has conducted many multi-media recruiting seminars, and has developed the acclaimed *Recruit-Me Athletic Scholarship System*.

He is the host of the weekly *Recruit-Me Athletic Scholarship Podcast*.

The Athletic Scholarship Recruiting Planner and Journal is a companion to Jon's book, *The Athletic Scholarship Playbook: A Step-by-Step Recruiting Roadmap for High School Athletes and Parents*. In the Playbook, he explains clearly what every family needs to know about recruiting and athletic scholarships. Jon delivers a step-by-step solution to landing a scholarship at the school of your choice. Find the book on Amazon in Kindle, paperback, and Audible formats.

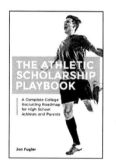

(Available in Kindle, paperback, and Audible formats)

amazon.com

Get on the right track with
THE ATHLETIC SCHOLARSHIP
RECRUITING PLANNER
AND JOURNAL

Made in the USA
Las Vegas, NV
30 January 2024